CW01651018

Standard Grade | General

Chemistry

General Level 2003

General Level 2004

General Level 2005

General Level 2006

General Level 2007

Leckie × Leckie

First exam published in 2003.
Published by Leckie & Leckie Ltd, 3rd Floor, 4 Queen Street, Edinburgh EH2 1JE
tel: 0131 220 6831 fax: 0131 225 9987 enquiries@leckieandleckie.co.uk www.leckieandleckie.co.uk

ISBN 978-1-84372-503-9

A CIP Catalogue record for this book is available from the British Library.

Printed in Scotland by Scotprint.

Leckie & Leckie is a division of Huveaux plc.

Leckie & Leckie is grateful to the copyright holders, as credited at the back of the book, for permission to use their material.
Every effort has been made to trace the copyright holders and to obtain their permission for the use of copyright material.
Leckie & Leckie will gladly receive information enabling them to rectify any error or omission in subsequent editions.

2003 | General

[BLANK PAGE]

FOR OFFICIAL USE

G

	KU	PS
Total Marks		

0500/401

NATIONAL QUALIFICATIONS 2003

FRIDAY, 23 MAY
9.00 AM – 10.30 AM

CHEMISTRY
STANDARD GRADE
General Level

Fill in these boxes and read what is printed below.

Full name of centre

Town

Forename(s)

Surname

Date of birth
Day Month Year

Scottish candidate number

Number of seat

1 All questions should be attempted.

2 Necessary data will be found in the Data Booklet provided for Chemistry at Standard Grade and Intermediate 2.

3 The questions may be answered in any order but all answers are to be written in this answer book, and must be written clearly and legibly in ink.

4 Rough work, if any should be necessary, as well as the fair copy, is to be written in this book.

Rough work should be scored through when the fair copy has been written.

5 Additional space for answers and rough work will be found at the end of the book.

6 The size of the space provided for an answer should not be taken as an indication of how much to write. It is not necessary to use all the space.

7 Before leaving the examination room you must give this book to the invigilator. If you do not, you may lose all the marks for this paper.

SCOTTISH QUALIFICATIONS AUTHORITY

PART 1

In Questions 1 to 8 of this part of the paper, an answer is given by circling the appropriate letter (or letters) in the answer grid provided.

In some questions, two letters are required for full marks.

If more than the correct number of answers is given, marks will be deducted.

In some cases, the number of correct responses is NOT identified in the question.

A total of 20 marks is available in this part of the paper.

SAMPLE QUESTION

A CH_4	B H_2	C CO_2
D CO	E C_2H_5OH	F C

(*a*) Identify the hydrocarbon(s).

Ⓐ	B	C
D	E	F

The one correct answer to part (*a*) is A. This should be circled.

(*b*) Identify the **two** elements.

A	Ⓑ	C
D	E	Ⓕ

As indicated in this question, there are **two** correct answers to part (*b*). These are B and F. Both answers are circled.

(*c*) Identify the substance(s) which can burn to produce **both** carbon dioxide and water.

Ⓐ	B	C
D	Ⓔ	F

There are **two** correct answers to part (*c*). These are A and E. Both answers are circled.

If, after you have recorded your answer, you decide that you have made an error and wish to make a change, you should cancel the original answer and circle the answer you now consider to be correct. Thus, in part (*a*), if you want to change an answer A to an answer D, your answer sheet would look like this:

~~Ⓐ~~	B	C
Ⓓ	E	F

If you want to change back to an answer which has already been scored out, you should enter a tick (✓) in the box of the answer of your choice, thus:

✓ ~~Ⓐ~~	B	C
~~Ⓓ~~	E	F

DO NOT WRITE IN THIS MARGIN

KU PS

1. The grid contains the names of some metals.
You may wish to use page 8 of the data booklet.

A magnesium	B lithium	C calcium
D nickel	E aluminium	F potassium

(*a*) Identify the metal which was discovered in 1827.

A	B	C
D	E	F

(*b*) Identify the transition metal.

A	B	C
D	E	F

[Turn over

DO NOT WRITE IN THIS MARGIN

KU	PS

2. There are many compounds of potassium.

A potassium sulphate	B potassium chloride
C potassium sulphite	D potassium nitrate

Identify the compound which does **not** contain oxygen.

A	B
C	D

3. The diagram shows part of the Periodic Table.

The letters do **not** represent the symbols for the elements.

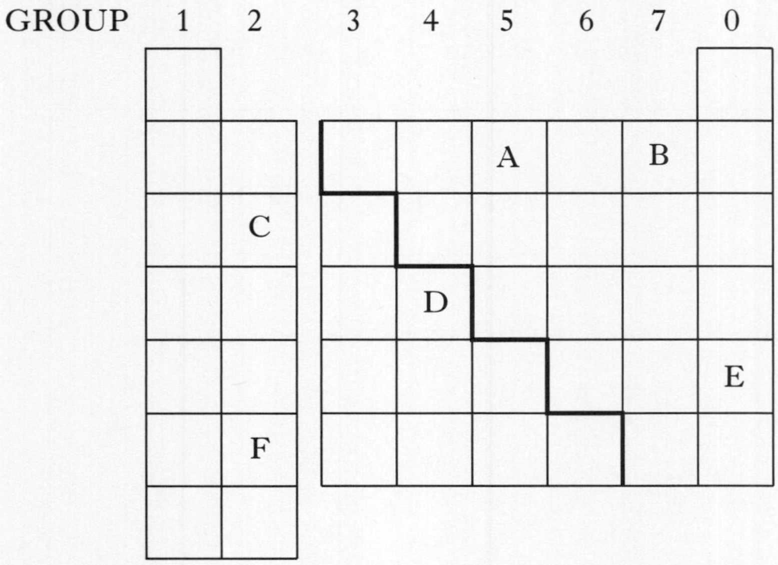

(*a*) Identify the element which has the electron arrangement 2, 5.

A	B	C	D	E	F

(*b*) Identify the **two** elements with similar chemical properties.

A	B	C	D	E	F

(*c*) Identify the noble gas.

A	B	C	D	E	F

[Turn over

DO NOT WRITE IN THIS MARGIN

KU PS

4. The grid contains the names of some chemical reactions and processes.

A combustion	B neutralisation	C polymerisation
D addition	E cracking	F electrolysis

(*a*) Identify the chemical reaction in which oxygen is used up.

A	B	C
D	E	F

(*b*) Identify the process in which a compound is broken down by electricity.

A	B	C
D	E	F

(*c*) Identify the chemical reaction in which glucose molecules join together to form starch.

A	B	C
D	E	F

DO NOT WRITE IN THIS MARGIN

KU | PS

5. Many solutions are used for chemical tests.

A iodine solution	B Benedict's reagent	C lime water
D bromine solution	E ferroxyl indicator	F pH indicator

(*a*) Identify the solution which is used to test for glucose.

A	B	C
D	E	F

(*b*) Identify the solution which is used to test for $Fe^{2+}(aq)$.

A	B	C
D	E	F

(*c*) Identify the solution which is used to test for a carbon to carbon double bond.

A	B	C
D	E	F

[Turn over

DO NOT WRITE IN THIS MARGIN

KU	PS

6. The grid contains the names of some non-metals.

A nitrogen	B carbon	C argon
D neon	E sulphur	F oxygen

(*a*) Identify the non-metal element which conducts electricity.

A	B	C
D	E	F

(*b*) Identify the gas which makes up about 20% of air.

A	B	C
D	E	F

(*c*) Identify the **two** gases which exist as diatomic molecules.

A	B	C
D	E	F

DO NOT WRITE IN THIS MARGIN

KU	PS

7. **Excess** copper carbonate was added to dilute hydrochloric acid in a beaker.

$CuCO_3(s) + 2HCl(aq) \rightarrow CuCl_2(aq) + CO_2(g) + H_2O(l)$

When the reaction had finished the contents of the beaker were filtered.

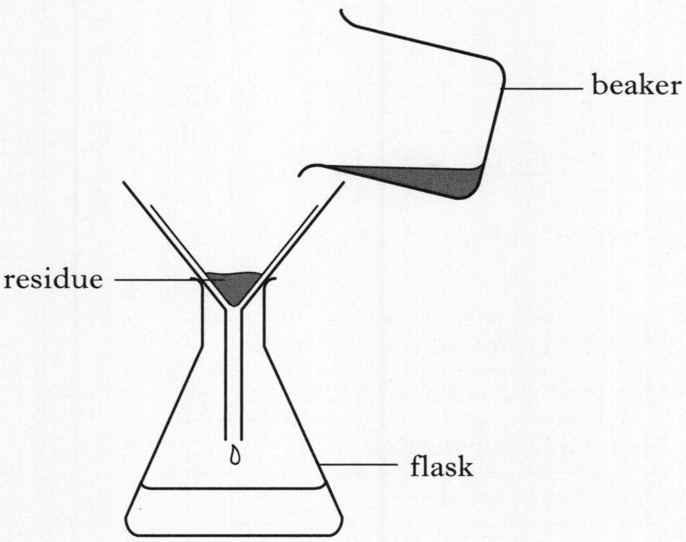

A	copper carbonate ($CuCO_3$)
B	hydrochloric acid (HCl)
C	copper chloride ($CuCl_2$)
D	carbon dioxide (CO_2)
E	water (H_2O)

(*a*) Identify the residue.

A
B
C
D
E

(*b*) Identify the substance(s) which collected in the flask.

A
B
C
D
E

8. Zinc reacts with dilute sulphuric acid.

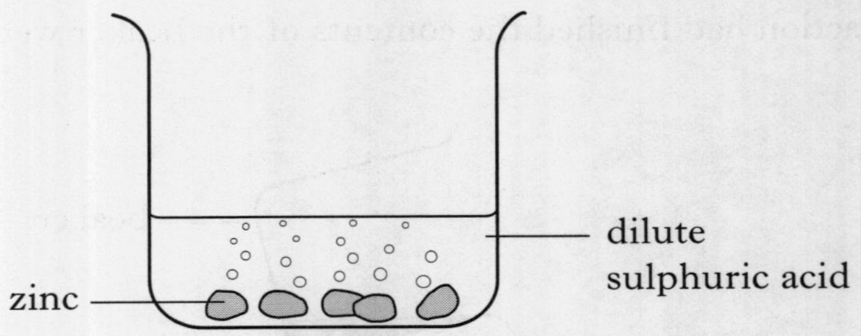

Identify the factor(s) which will speed up the reaction.

A	Using a larger volume of acid
B	Diluting the acid with water
C	Using a larger beaker
D	Heating the acid
E	Using a catalyst

A
B
C
D
E

DO NOT WRITE IN THIS MARGIN

Marks	KU	PS

PART 2

A total of 40 marks is available in this part of the paper.

9. Copper can be mixed with other metals to produce alloys for different uses.

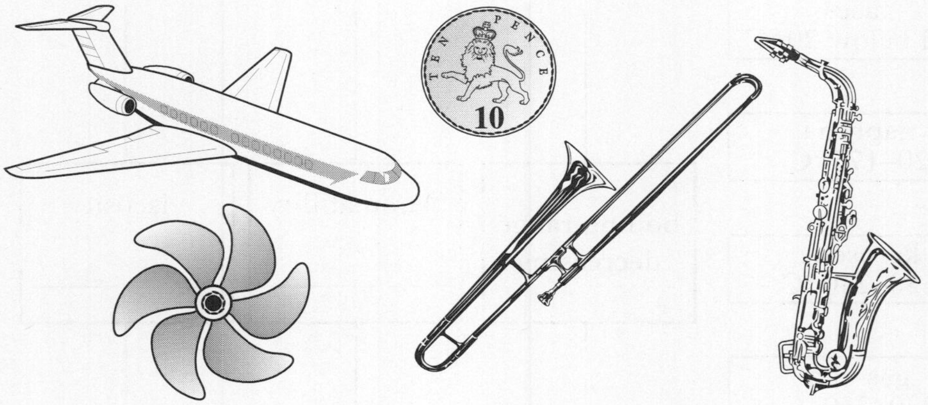

Aluminium is added to copper to make an alloy suitable for aircraft bodies. Coins are made from a hard wearing alloy which contains copper and nickel. Musical instruments can be made from an alloy of copper and zinc. If tin is added to copper the alloy can be used to make ships' propellers.

(*a*) Present this information in a table with suitable headings. **2**

(*b*) Copper metal is a finite resource.

What is meant by the term "finite resource"?

____

____ **1**

(3)

DO NOT WRITE IN THIS MARGIN

Marks KU PS

10. (*a*) The diagram shows the names and boiling ranges of some of the fractions which are obtained from crude oil.

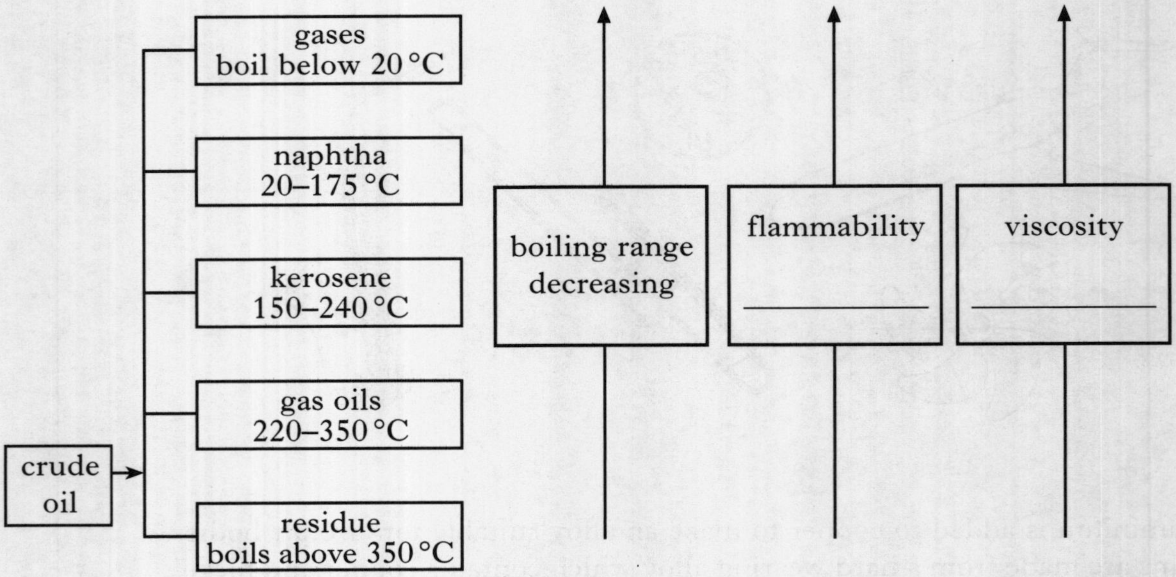

(i) Name the process which is used to separate the crude oil into fractions.

______________________________ **1**

(ii) On the diagram, label the arrows for flammability and viscosity as either **increasing** or **decreasing**. **1**

(iii) In which fraction is propane found?
You may wish to use page 6 of the data booklet.

______________________________ **1**

DO NOT WRITE IN THIS MARGIN

Marks KU PS

10. (continued)

(*b*) Decane is a compound found in the kerosene fraction.

To which family of hydrocarbons does decane belong?

____ **1**

(*c*) Decane can be broken down into a mixture of saturated and unsaturated hydrocarbons.

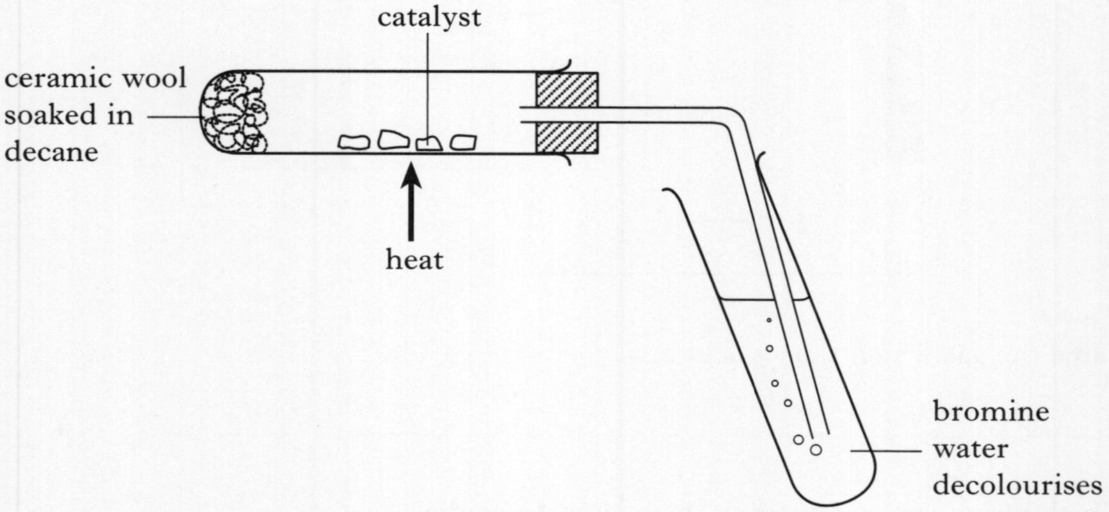

(i) What is meant by a **saturated** hydrocarbon?

____

____ **1**

(ii) Decane can break down in the following way:

$C_{10}H_{22} \rightarrow C_7H_{16} + \mathbf{X}$

Write down the molecular formula for **X**.

________________________ **1**

(6)

[Turn over

DO NOT WRITE IN THIS MARGIN

Marks | KU | PS

11. Fish cannot survive in lochs if acid rain makes the pH of the water too low.

(*a*) Name the gas which causes acid rain.

______________________________________ **1**

(*b*) Which ion causes the water in the loch to be acidic?

______________________________________ **1**

(*c*) Name a substance which could be added to the loch to increase the pH of the water.

______________________________________ **1**

(3)

DO NOT WRITE IN THIS MARGIN

Marks KU PS

12. The pie chart shows the composition of the Earth's crust.

Composition of the Earth's crust

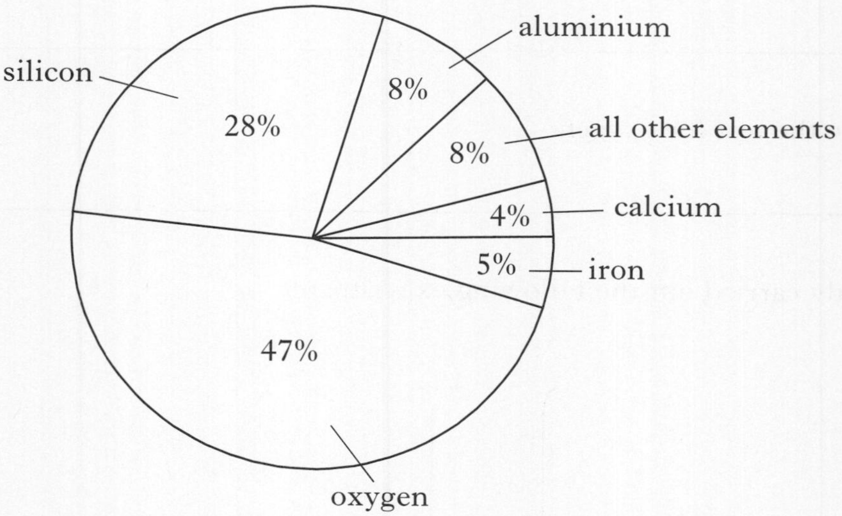

(*a*) Present the information as a bar chart.

Use appropriate scales to fill most of the graph paper.

(Additional graph paper, if required, can be found on page 25.)

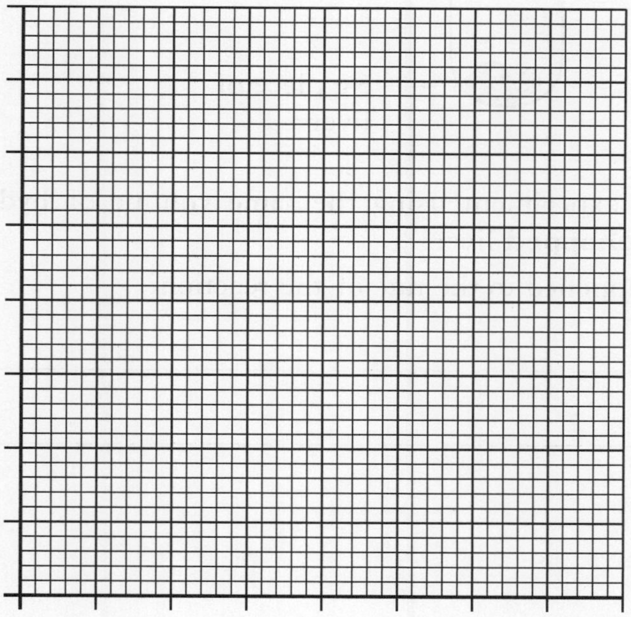

2

(*b*) Sand is a compound made from the two most common elements in the Earth's crust.

Write the chemical formula for sand.

____ **1**

(3)

DO NOT WRITE IN THIS MARGIN

Marks | KU | PS

13. The liver is an organ found in the human body. It contains the enzyme catalase which helps break down hydrogen peroxide into water and oxygen.

(*a*) What is meant by the term "enzyme"?

____ **1**

(*b*) State the test for oxygen.

____ **1**

(*c*) Sandy carried out the following experiment.

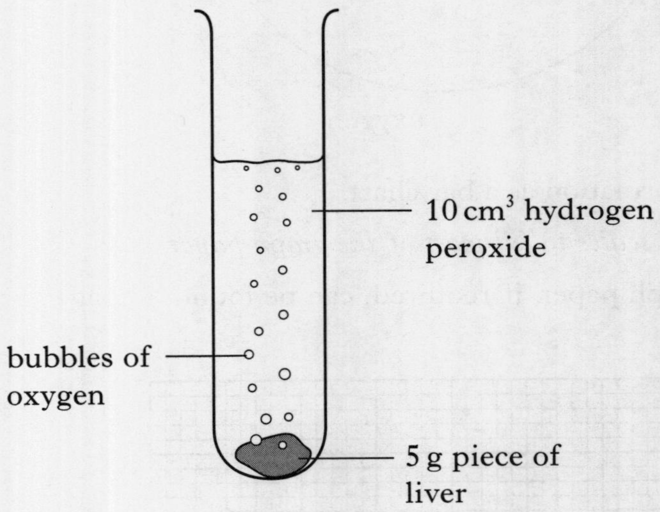

Sandy repeated the experiment using the same volume of hydrogen peroxide and 5 g of **chopped** liver.

What would have happened to the rate of the reaction?

____

____ **1**

DO NOT WRITE IN THIS MARGIN

Marks | KU | PS

13. (continued)

(*d*) Sandy also investigated the activity of catalase at different temperatures. His results are shown on the graph.

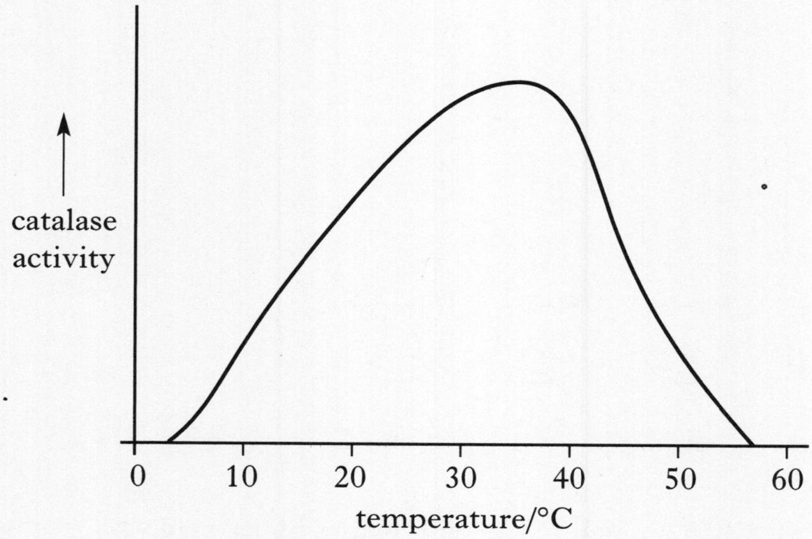

What effect does increasing the temperature from 20 °C to 50 °C have on the activity of the catalase?

____

____ **1**

(4)

[Turn over

DO NOT WRITE IN THIS MARGIN

Marks | KU | PS

14. The reactivity of metals can be compared by adding them to a mixture of hydrochloric acid and detergent.

Amy set up five test tubes each containing a different metal.

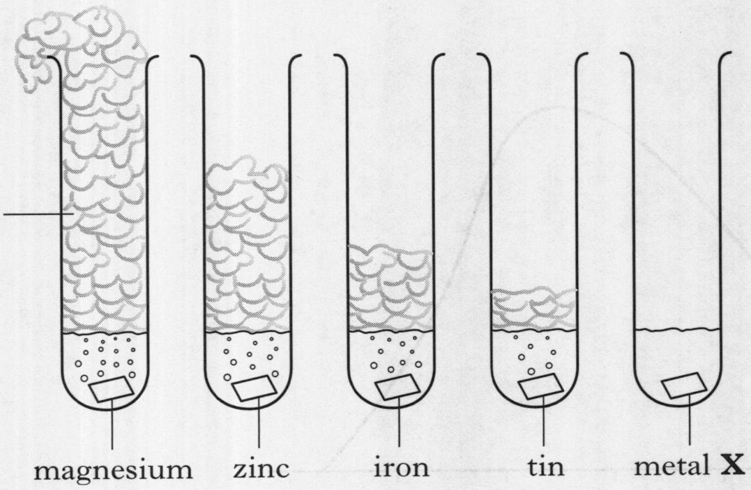

(*a*) Name the gas produced when a metal reacts with hydrochloric acid.

______________________________ **1**

(*b*) Suggest a name for metal **X**.

You may wish to use page 7 of the data booklet.

______________________________ **1**

(*c*) Name one factor which Amy would have kept the same to ensure a fair comparison.

______________________________ **1**

(3)

DO NOT WRITE IN THIS MARGIN

Marks | KU | PS

15. Ethene is used to make a variety of products. Some of these are shown below.

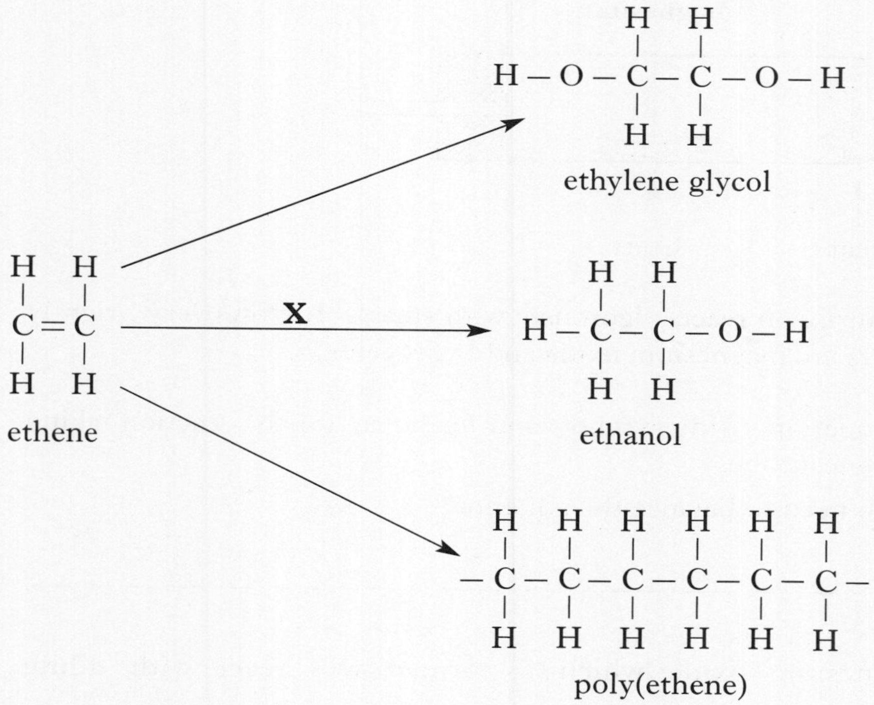

(*a*) Write the molecular formula for ethylene glycol.

____ **1**

(*b*) Name substance **X**.

____ **1**

(*c*) Poly(ethene) is a **synthetic** polymer. What does **synthetic** mean?

____ **1**

(3)

[Turn over

DO NOT WRITE IN THIS MARGIN

Marks KU PS

16.

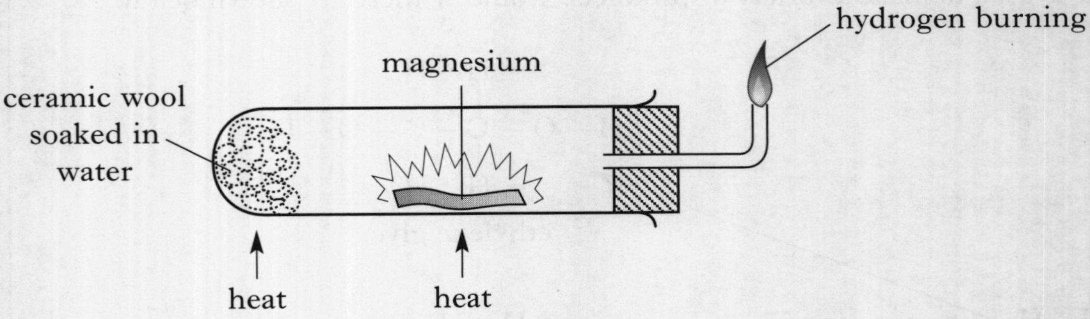

Hot magnesium ribbon reacts vigorously with steam. It glows very brightly and the products are magnesium oxide and hydrogen gas.

(*a*) Write an equation, using symbols and formulae, for the reaction taking place in the test tube.

There is no need to balance the equation.

____ **1**

(*b*) The magnesium oxide which is formed will react with dilute hydrochloric acid.

Name the type of chemical reaction which takes place.

____ **1**

(*c*) Name the product formed when hydrogen burns.

____ **1**

(3)

DO NOT WRITE IN THIS MARGIN

Marks | KU | PS

17. The diagram shows a copper/zinc cell.

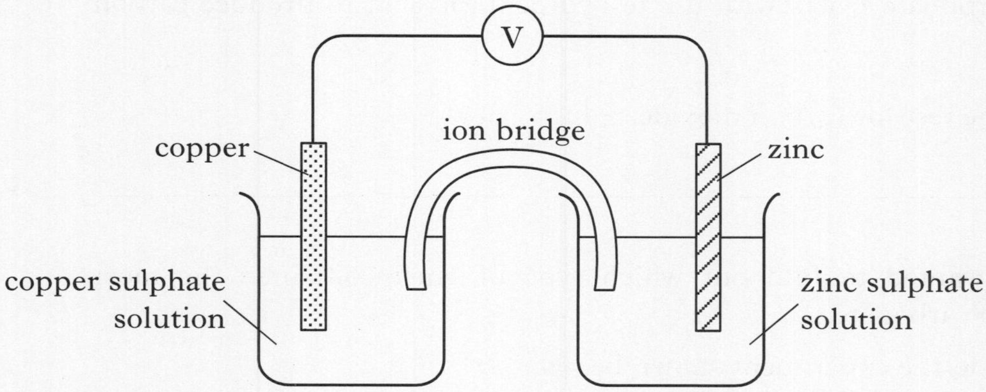

(*a*) In the cell, the electricity flows through the wires from the zinc to the copper.

Name the type of charged particle that flows through the **wires**.

________________________________ **1**

(*b*) What is the purpose of the ion bridge?

________________________________ **1**

(*c*) Eventually the cell would stop producing electricity.

Give a reason for this.

____

________________________________ **1**

(*d*) Name a metal which could replace zinc to produce a larger voltage.

You may wish to use page 7 of the data booklet.

________________________________ **1**

(4)

[Turn over

DO NOT WRITE IN THIS MARGIN

Marks | KU | PS

18. Egg shells and sea shells contain calcium carbonate.

Calcium carbonate reacts with dilute hydrochloric acid to produce carbon dioxide gas.

(*a*) State the test for carbon dioxide.

______________________________ **1**

(*b*) Adam wanted to find out which type of shell contained the most calcium carbonate.

He set up the experiment shown below.

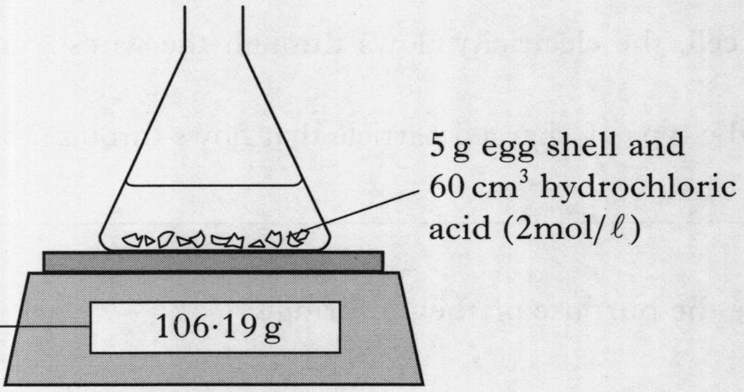

(i) State **two** ways in which Adam would know when the reaction had finished.

____

______________________________ **2**

(ii) Adam repeated the experiment using 5 g sea shell. His results are shown in the table.

	Sea shell	**Egg shell**
Balance reading at start/g	106.19	106.19
Balance reading at end/g	104.22	104.01

Which type of shell contained the most calcium carbonate?

______________________________ **1**

(4)

DO NOT WRITE IN THIS MARGIN

Marks KU PS

19. **The Manufacture of Sulphuric Acid**

Molten sulphur is sprayed into a furnace and burned in air. This produces a mixture of sulphur dioxide and air which then passes into a catalyst chamber where sulphur trioxide is formed. The sulphur trioxide is reacted with concentrated sulphuric acid in an absorber to produce superconcentrated sulphuric acid.

Use this information to complete the flow diagram.

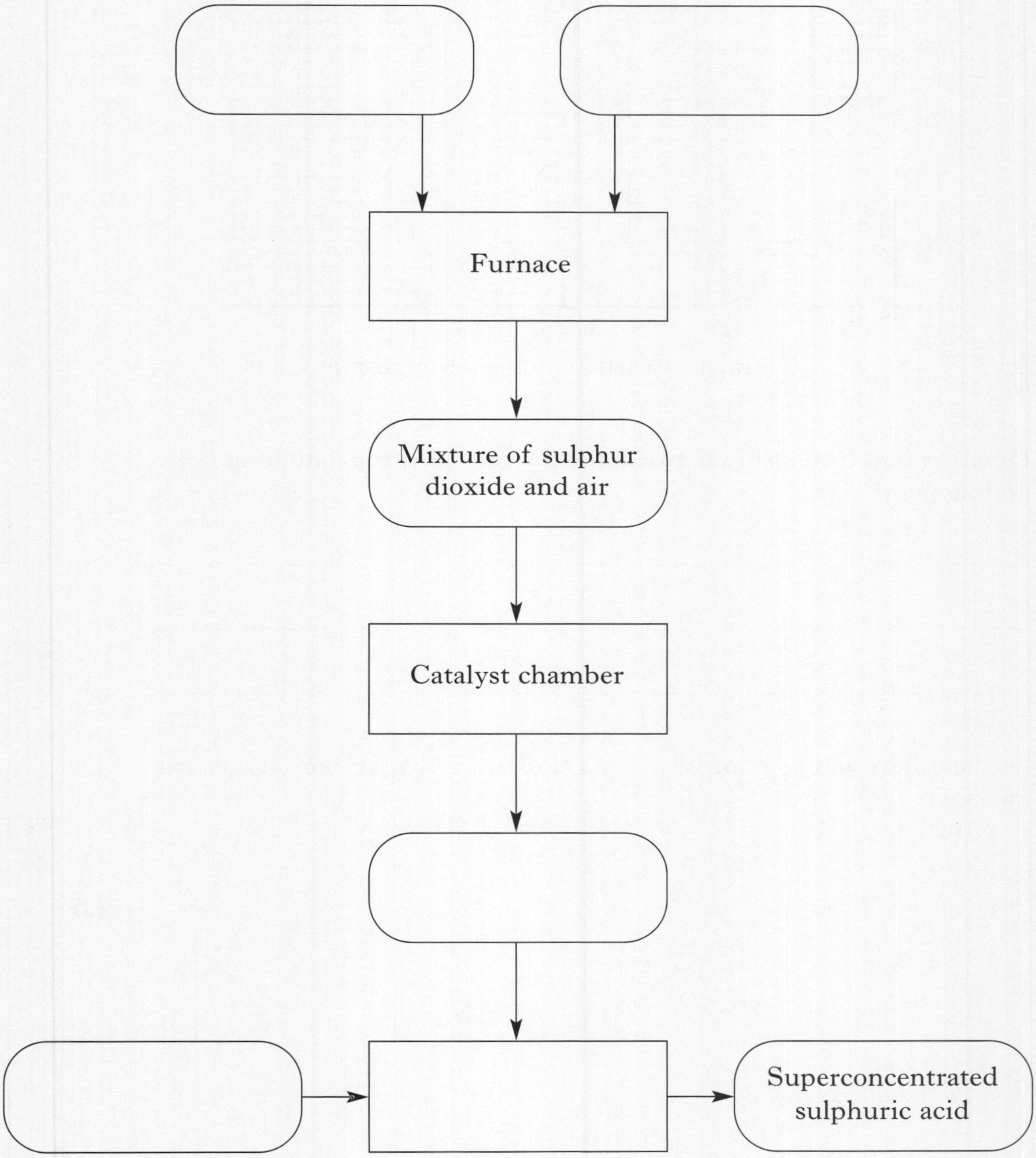

(2)

[Turn over

DO NOT WRITE IN THIS MARGIN

Marks KU PS

20. The bar chart shows the boiling points of some alcohols.

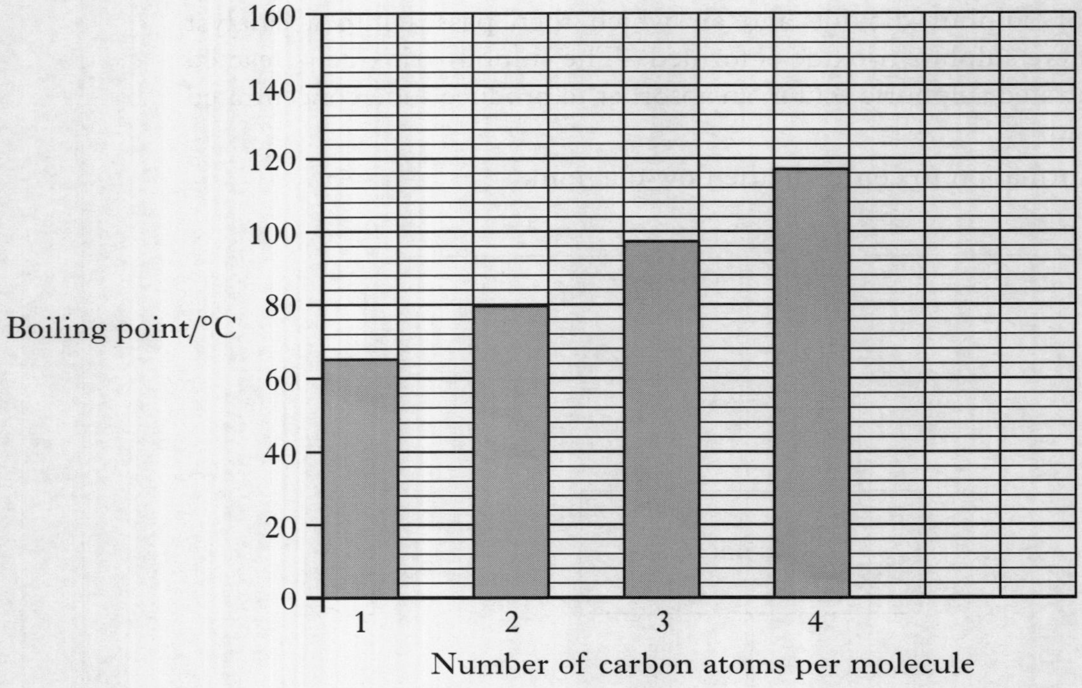

(*a*) Describe the relationship between the number of carbon atoms and the boiling point.

____

____

____ **1**

(*b*) Predict the boiling point of the alcohol with five carbon atoms per molecule.

________ °C **1**

(2)

[*END OF QUESTION PAPER*]

DO NOT WRITE IN THIS MARGIN

KU PS

ADDITIONAL SPACE FOR ANSWERS

ADDITIONAL GRAPH PAPER FOR QUESTION 12(*a*)

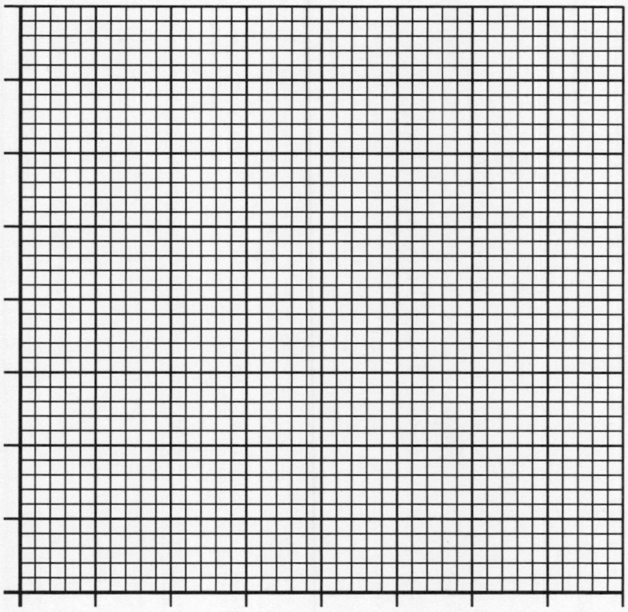

DO NOT WRITE IN THIS MARGIN

KU	PS

ADDITIONAL SPACE FOR ANSWERS

2004 | General

[BLANK PAGE]

FOR OFFICIAL USE

G

	KU	PS
Total Marks		

0500/401

NATIONAL QUALIFICATIONS 2004

MONDAY, 10 MAY
9.00 AM – 10.30 AM

CHEMISTRY
STANDARD GRADE
General Level

Fill in these boxes and read what is printed below.

Full name of centre

Town

Forename(s)

Surname

Date of birth

Day Month Year

Scottish candidate number

Number of seat

1 All questions should be attempted.

2 Necessary data will be found in the Data Booklet provided for Chemistry at Standard Grade and Intermediate 2.

3 The questions may be answered in any order but all answers are to be written in this answer book, and must be written clearly and legibly in ink.

4 Rough work, if any should be necessary, as well as the fair copy, is to be written in this book.

Rough work should be scored through when the fair copy has been written.

5 Additional space for answers and rough work will be found at the end of the book.

6 The size of the space provided for an answer should not be taken as an indication of how much to write. It is not necessary to use all the space.

7 Before leaving the examination room you must give this book to the invigilator. If you do not, you may lose all the marks for this paper.

SCOTTISH QUALIFICATIONS AUTHORITY

SAB 0500/401 6/26170

PART 1

In Questions 1 to 8 of this part of the paper, an answer is given by circling the appropriate letter (or letters) in the answer grid provided.

In some questions, two letters are required for full marks.

If more than the correct number of answers is given, marks will be deducted.

A total of 20 marks is available in this part of the paper.

SAMPLE QUESTION

A CH_4	B H_2	C CO_2
D CO	E C_2H_5OH	F C

(*a*) Identify the hydrocarbon.

(A)	B	C
D	E	F

The correct answer to part (*a*) is A. This should be circled.

(*b*) Identify the **two** elements.

A	(B)	C
D	E	(F)

As indicated in this question, there are **two** correct answers to part (*b*). These are B and F. Both answers are circled.

If, after you have recorded your answer, you decide that you have made an error and wish to make a change, you should cancel the original answer and circle the answer you now consider to be correct. Thus, in part (*a*), if you want to change an answer A to an answer D, your answer sheet would look like this:

~~(A)~~	B	C
(D)	E	F

If you want to change back to an answer which has already been scored out, you should enter a tick (✓) in the box of the answer of your choice, thus:

✓ ~~(A)~~	B	C
~~(D)~~	E	F

DO NOT WRITE IN THIS MARGIN

Marks KU PS

1. The grid contains the names of some elements.

A neon	B lithium	C chlorine
D oxygen	E copper	F argon

(*a*) Identify the alkali metal.

A	B	C
D	E	F

1

(*b*) Identify the element with the highest melting point.
You may wish to use page 3 of the data booklet to help you.

A	B	C
D	E	F

1

(*c*) Identify the **two** very unreactive elements.

A	B	C
D	E	F

1

(3)

[Turn over

DO NOT WRITE IN THIS MARGIN

Marks | KU | PS

2. Hydrocarbons are compounds containing hydrogen and carbon only.

A CH_4	B C_2H_4	C C_6H_{14}
D C_5H_{12}	E C_3H_8	F C_4H_8

(*a*) Identify the molecular formula for pentane.

A	B	C
D	E	F

1

(*b*) Identify the **two** molecular formulae which represent alkenes.

A	B	C
D	E	F

1

(*c*) Identify the hydrocarbon which has a boiling point of 69 °C.

You may wish to use page 6 of the data booklet to help you.

A	B	C
D	E	F

1

(3)

DO NOT WRITE IN THIS MARGIN

Marks KU PS

3. The grid contains the names of some metals.

A zinc	B calcium	C iron
D magnesium	E silver	F sodium

(*a*) Identify the metal which is used as the catalyst in the Haber process.

A	B	C
D	E	F

1

(*b*) Identify the metal which does **not** react with dilute acid.

A	B	C
D	E	F

1

(2)

[Turn over

DO NOT WRITE IN THIS MARGIN

Marks KU PS

4. The grid contains the names of some elements.

A hydrogen	B aluminium	C carbon
D nitrogen	E phosphorus	F fluorine

(*a*) Identify the non-metal element which can conduct electricity.

A	B	C
D	E	F

1

(*b*) Identify the **two** elements which plants obtain from fertilisers.

A	B	C
D	E	F

1

(*c*) Identify the element which is present in all acids.

A	B	C
D	E	F

1

(3)

DO NOT WRITE IN THIS MARGIN

Marks KU PS

5. The grid contains the names of some gases.

A oxygen	B hydrogen	C helium
D nitrogen	E chlorine	F xenon

(*a*) Identify the gas which makes up approximately 80% of the air.

A	B	C
D	E	F

1

(*b*) Identify the **two** gases which do **not** exist as diatomic molecules.

A	B	C
D	E	F

1

(2)

[Turn over

DO NOT WRITE IN THIS MARGIN

Marks | KU | PS

6. The grid contains the names of some processes.

A respiration	B cracking	C distillation
D filtration	E photosynthesis	F galvanising

(*a*) Identify the process which produces water and carbon dioxide.

A	B	C
D	E	F

1

(*b*) Identify the process which can be used to separate alcohol and water.

A	B	C
D	E	F

1

(2)

DO NOT WRITE IN THIS MARGIN

Marks | KU | PS

7. Metals and their compounds take part in many reactions.

A	Fe_2O_3	+ 3CO	⟶	2Fe	+ $3CO_2$
B	2Mg	+ SiO_2	⟶	2MgO	+ Si
C	$CuCO_3$		⟶	CuO	+ CO_2
D	2Zn	+ O_2	⟶	2ZnO	

(*a*) Identify the reaction which takes place in the blast furnace.

A
B
C
D

1

(*b*) Identify the reaction which produces a non-metal element.

A
B
C
D

1

(2)

[Turn over

DO NOT WRITE IN THIS MARGIN

Marks KU PS

8. Lorraine added magnesium carbonate to dilute hydrochloric acid in a beaker until no more reacted.

$$MgCO_3(s) + 2HCl(aq) \longrightarrow MgCl_2(aq) + CO_2(g) + H_2O(\ell)$$

The contents of the beaker were then filtered.

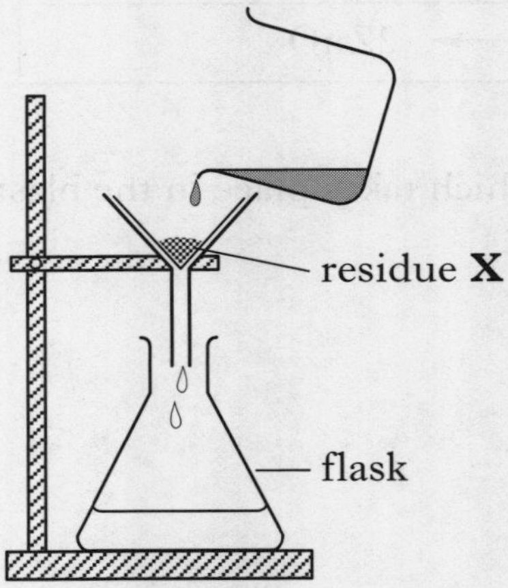

A	magnesium carbonate,	$MgCO_3$
B	hydrochloric acid,	HCl
C	magnesium chloride,	$MgCl_2$
D	carbon dioxide,	CO_2
E	water,	H_2O

(*a*) Identify the residue **X**.

A
B
C
D
E

1

(*b*) Identify the **two** substances which collected in the flask.

A
B
C
D
E

2

(3)

DO NOT WRITE IN THIS MARGIN

Marks KU PS

PART 2

A total of 40 marks is available in this part of the paper.

9. Coal is an example of a fossil fuel.

(*a*) What is meant by a **fuel**?

____

____ **1**

(*b*) Describe how coal was formed.

____

____

____

____

____

____ **2**

(*c*) Give another example of a fossil fuel.

____ **1**

(4)

[Turn over

DO NOT WRITE IN THIS MARGIN

Marks KU PS

10. The diagram shows some ways in which iron can be protected from rusting.

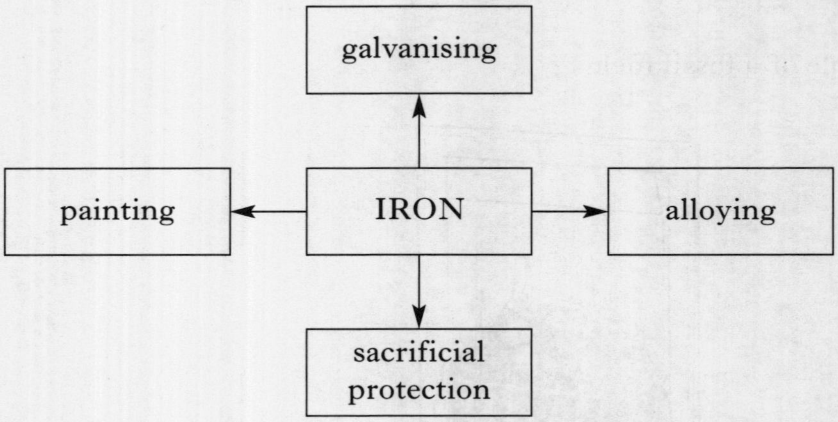

(*a*) Name a metal which is suitable for the sacrificial protection of iron.

______________________________ **1**

(*b*) Which metal is used to galvanise iron?

______________________________ **1**

(*c*) How does painting prevent the rusting of iron?

____

____ **1**

(*d*) Alloys of iron are called steels.
Name **another** alloy.

______________________________ **1**

(4)

DO NOT WRITE IN THIS MARGIN

Marks | KU | PS

11. Some plastic bags are made from a synthetic polymer called polythene.

(*a*) What is meant by the term **synthetic**?

____

____ **1**

(*b*) Draw a section of polythene, showing 3 monomer units joined together.

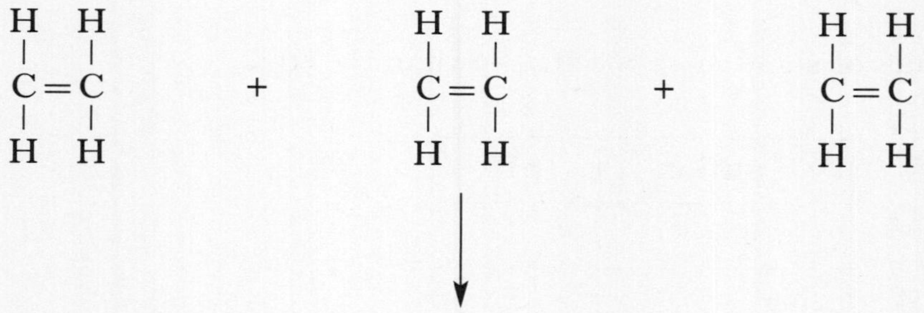

1

(*c*) Polythene is not biodegradable.

What is meant by **biodegradable**?

____

____

____ **1**

(3)

[Turn over

DO NOT WRITE IN THIS MARGIN

Marks | KU | PS

12. The pH of a solution can be found using a pH meter.

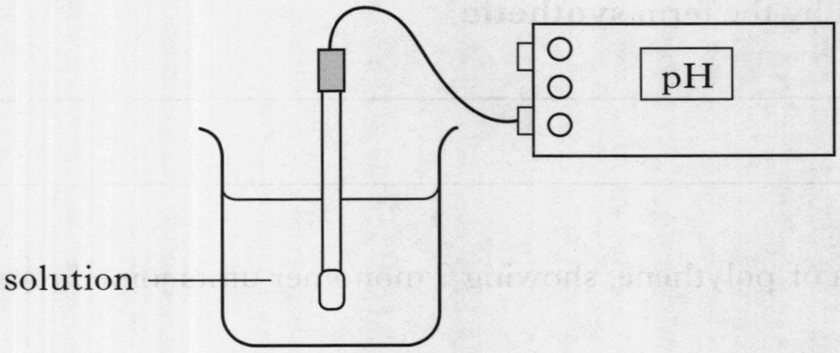

The pH values of some solutions are shown in the table.

Solution	pH
vinegar	3
cola	5
fruit juice	5
bleach	9
detergent	8

(*a*) Name the **two** alkaline solutions in the table.

____

____ **1**

Marks | KU | PS

12. (continued)

(*b*) Draw a bar graph to show the information in the table.

Use appropriate scales to fill most of the graph paper.

(Additional graph paper, if required, can be found on page 24.)

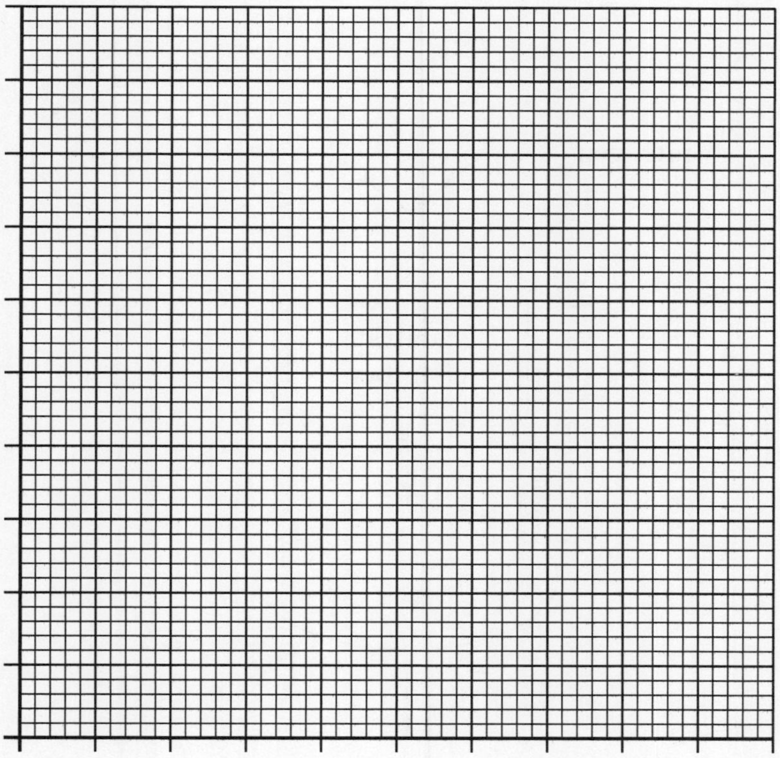

2

(3)

[Turn over

DO NOT WRITE IN THIS MARGIN

Marks	KU	PS

13. Ammonium nitrate is made by the reaction of ammonia with nitric acid.

Ammonia is made by passing a mixture of nitrogen and hydrogen through a catalyst chamber. Unreacted nitrogen and hydrogen are removed and returned to the catalyst chamber. The ammonia gas then enters a reaction vessel in which ammonium nitrate is produced.

(*a*) Use this information to complete the flow diagram.

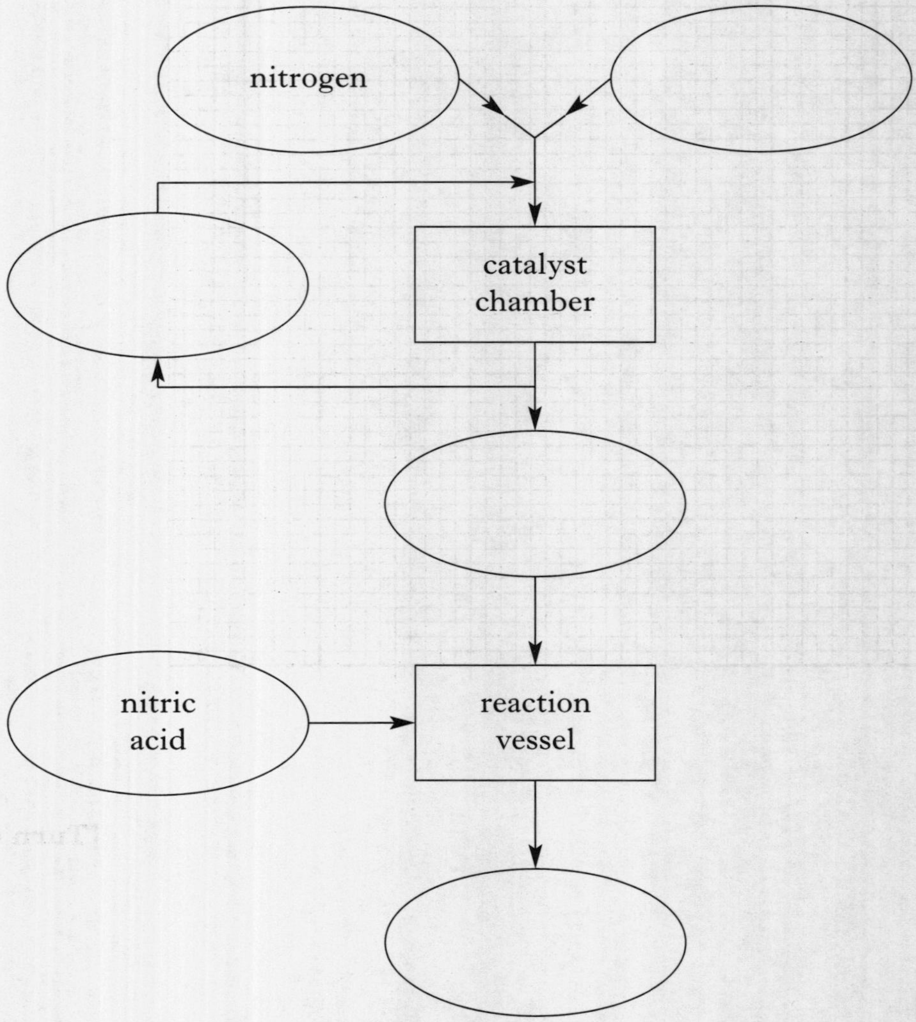

2

DO NOT WRITE IN THIS MARGIN

Marks KU PS

13. (continued)

(*b*) The pie chart shows the uses of ammonia.

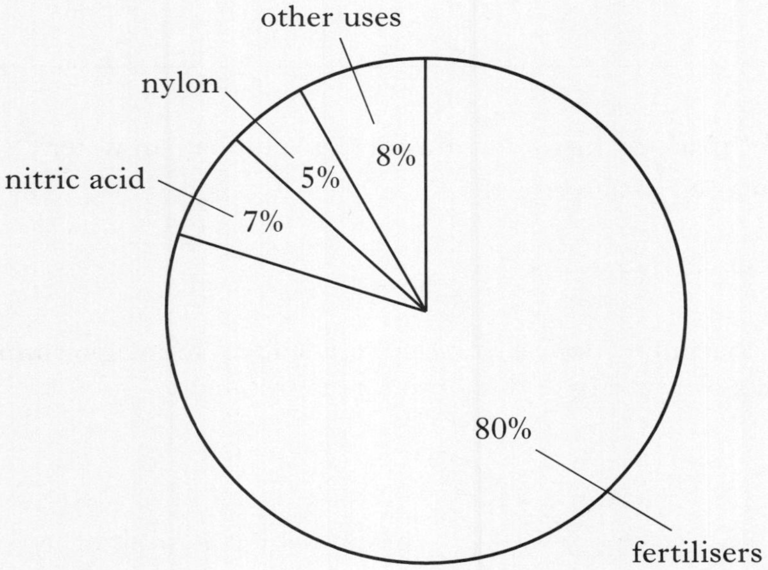

Present this information as a table with suitable headings.

2

(4)

[Turn over

DO NOT WRITE IN THIS MARGIN

Marks | KU | PS

14. Magnesium sulphate is a compound present in Epsom Salts.

(*a*) Name the elements present in magnesium sulphate.

____

____ **1**

(*b*) A **solution** can be made by dissolving magnesium sulphate in water. What term can be used to describe the water?

________________________ **1**

(*c*) When drops of barium chloride solution are added to magnesium sulphate solution a solid forms and the mixture turns cloudy.

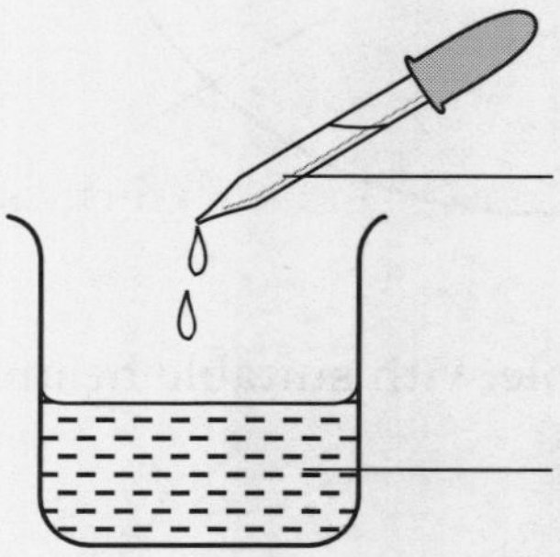

(i) What type of chemical reaction takes place?

________________________ **1**

(ii) Name the solid formed in this reaction.
You may wish to use page 5 of the data booklet to help you.

____ **1**

(4)

DO NOT WRITE IN THIS MARGIN

Marks KU PS

15. Pairs of metals can be used to produce a cell.

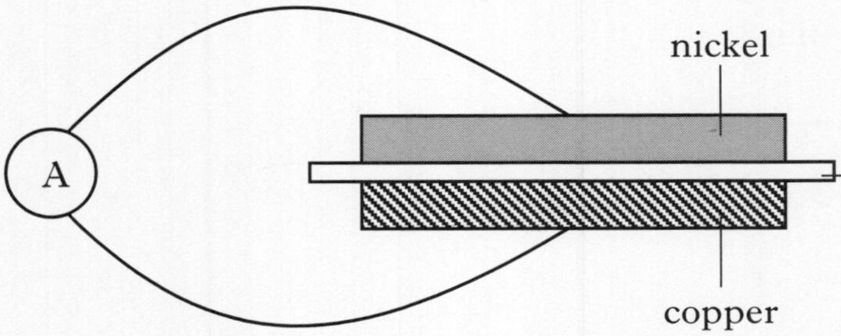

(*a*) What is the purpose of the filter paper soaked in sodium chloride solution?

____

____ **1**

(*b*) **On the wires**, indicate the direction of electron flow. **1**

(*c*) Give the name of a metal which could replace the nickel and cause the electrons to flow in the opposite direction.

______________________ **1**

(*d*) Cells are used in calculators and watches.

Give a **disadvantage** of a cell compared with mains electricity.

____

____ **1**

(4)

[Turn over

DO NOT WRITE IN THIS MARGIN

Marks | KU | PS

16. Heptane can be cracked using aluminium oxide as the catalyst.

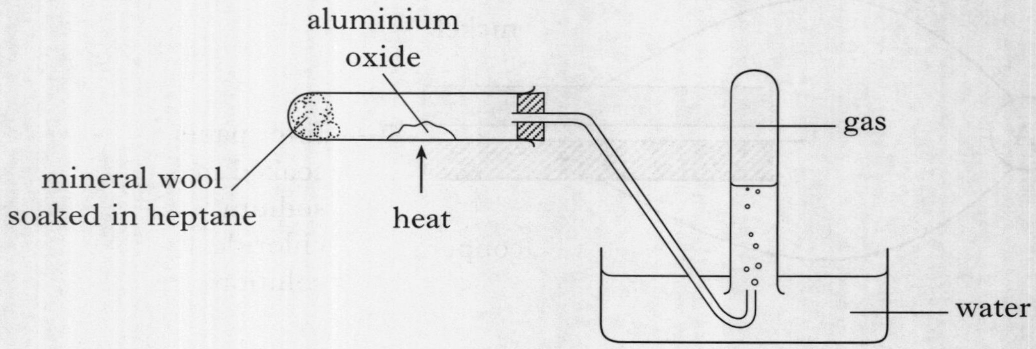

One of the reactions which takes place is

$$\underset{\text{heptane}}{C_7H_{16}(\ell)} \longrightarrow C_3H_6(g) + \mathbf{X}$$

(*a*) Draw the full structural formula for **heptane**. **1**

(*b*) Write the molecular formula for **X**.

______________________________ **1**

(*c*) Name the product C_3H_6.

______________________________ **1**

(*d*) Aluminium oxide is a white solid but at the end of the experiment it is covered in a black substance.

Suggest what the black substance could be.

______________________________ **1**

(4)

DO NOT WRITE IN THIS MARGIN

Marks KU PS

17. When Matthew added manganese dioxide to hydrogen peroxide solution, oxygen was produced.

Manganese dioxide is a catalyst.

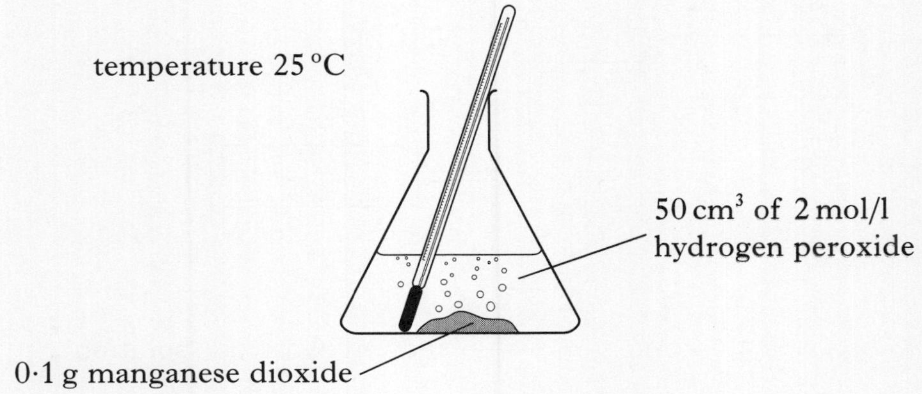

(*a*) (i) What is the purpose of a catalyst?

____ **1**

(ii) What will be the mass of the manganese dioxide at the end of the reaction?

__________ g **1**

(*b*) He then wanted to see if raising the temperature to 35 °C would speed up the reaction.

Complete the labelling of the diagram to show how he would make his second experiment a fair test.

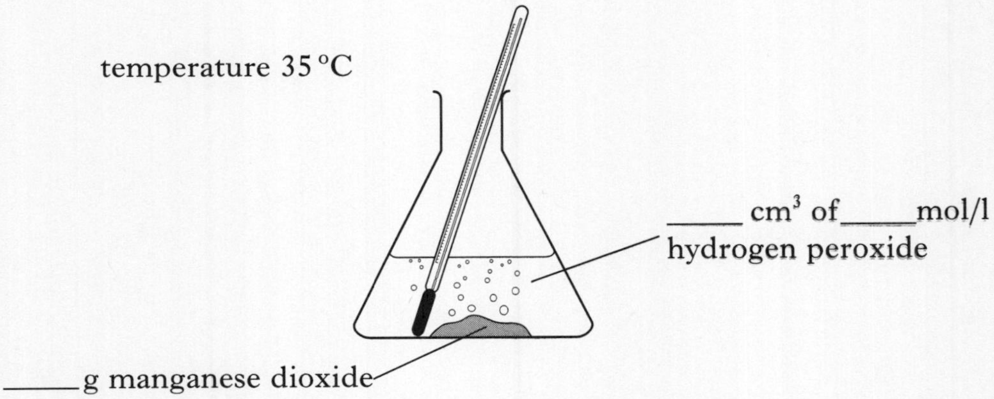

1

(3)

[Turn over

DO NOT WRITE IN THIS MARGIN

Marks | KU | PS

18. A chemist used the following apparatus to investigate biogas. Biogas is a mixture of carbon dioxide and methane.

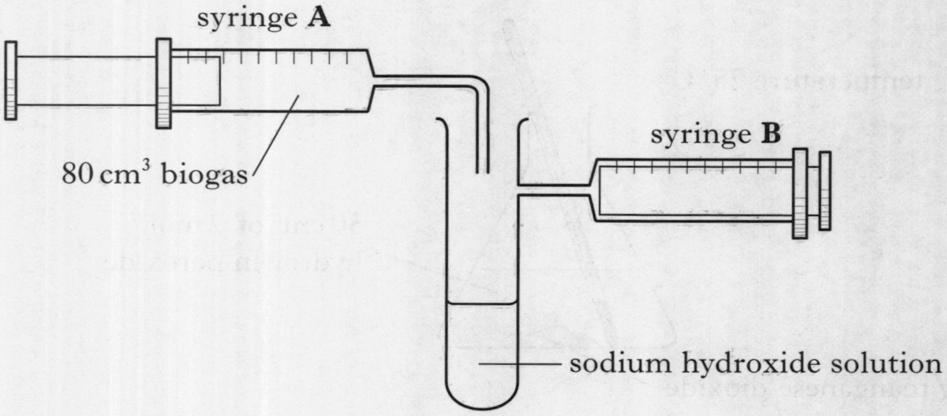

80 cm^3 of biogas was bubbled into the sodium hydroxide solution which removed the carbon dioxide. The remaining gas was collected in syringe **B**.

(*a*) Complete the diagram to show how the biogas was passed into the sodium hydroxide solution. **2**

(*b*) She found that the biogas contained 60% carbon dioxide and 40% methane.

What volume of gas was collected in syringe **B**?

__________ cm^3 **1**

(3)

DO NOT WRITE IN THIS MARGIN

Marks | KU | PS

19. Starch and glucose are carbohydrates.

(*a*) Which chemical would you use to test for starch?

____ **1**

(*b*) What is the chemical name for the alcohol produced by the fermentation of glucose?

____ **1**

(*c*) The percentage of alcohol in a wine depends on the temperature of the fermentation process. Some results are shown on the graph.

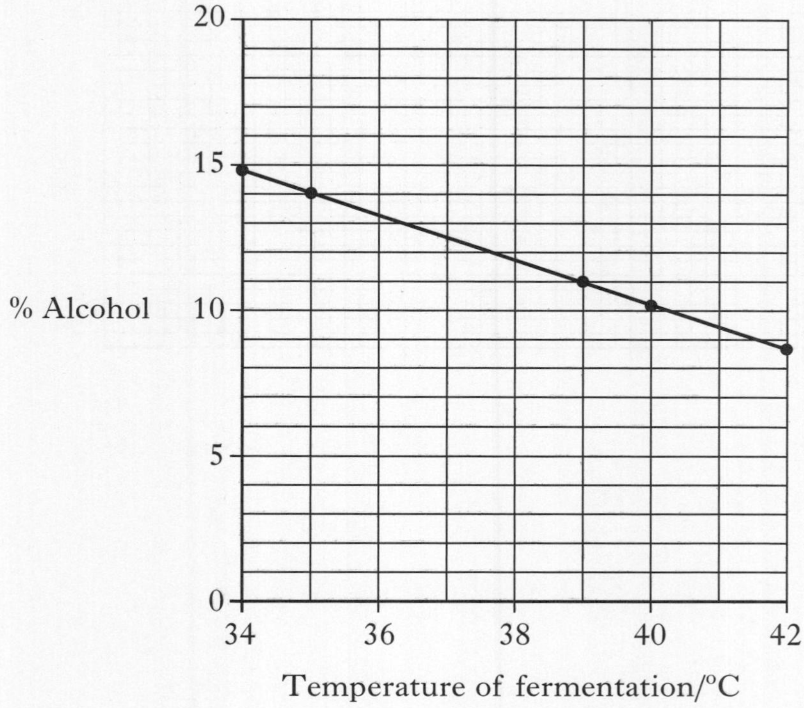

(i) Describe how the temperature of fermentation affects the % alcohol produced.

____

____

____ **1**

(ii) Use the graph to estimate the % alcohol when the temperature is 37 °C.

__________ % **1**

(4)

[*END OF QUESTION PAPER*]

ADDITIONAL SPACE FOR ANSWERS

ADDITIONAL GRAPH PAPER FOR QUESTION 12(*b*)

2005 | General

[BLANK PAGE]

FOR OFFICIAL USE

G

	KU	PS
Total Marks		

0500/401

NATIONAL QUALIFICATIONS 2005

MONDAY, 9 MAY
9.00 AM – 10.30 AM

CHEMISTRY
STANDARD GRADE
General Level

Fill in these boxes and read what is printed below.

Full name of centre

Town

Forename(s)

Surname

Date of birth
Day Month Year

Scottish candidate number

Number of seat

1 All questions should be attempted.

2 Necessary data will be found in the Data Booklet provided for Chemistry at Standard Grade and Intermediate 2.

3 The questions may be answered in any order but all answers are to be written in this answer book, and must be written clearly and legibly in ink.

4 Rough work, if any should be necessary, as well as the fair copy, is to be written in this book.
Rough work should be scored through when the fair copy has been written.

5 Additional space for answers and rough work will be found at the end of the book.

6 The size of the space provided for an answer should not be taken as an indication of how much to write. It is not necessary to use all the space.

7 Before leaving the examination room you must give this book to the invigilator. If you do not, you may lose all the marks for this paper.

SCOTTISH QUALIFICATIONS AUTHORITY

SAB 0500/401 6/28670

PART 1

In Questions 1 to 8 of this part of the paper, an answer is given by circling the appropriate letter (or letters) in the answer grid provided.

In some questions, two letters are required for full marks.

If more than the correct number of answers is given, marks will be deducted.

A total of 20 marks is available in this part of the paper.

SAMPLE QUESTION

A CH_4	B H_2	C CO_2
D CO	E C_2H_5OH	F C

(*a*) Identify the hydrocarbon.

(A)	B	C
D	E	F

The one correct answer to part (*a*) is A. This should be circled.

(*b*) Identify the **two** elements.

A	(B)	C
D	E	(F)

As indicated in this question, there are **two** correct answers to part (*b*). These are B and F. Both answers are circled.

If, after you have recorded your answer, you decide that you have made an error and wish to make a change, you should cancel the original answer and circle the answer you now consider to be correct. Thus, in part (*a*), if you want to change an answer A to an answer D, your answer sheet would look like this:

~~(A)~~	B	C
(D)	E	F

If you want to change back to an answer which has already been scored out, you should enter a tick (✓) in the box of the answer of your choice, thus:

✓ ~~(A)~~	B	C
~~(D)~~	E	F

DO NOT WRITE IN THIS MARGIN

Marks KU PS

1. The names of some elements are shown.

A zinc	B magnesium	C sulphur
D sodium	E carbon	F copper

(*a*) Identify the element with the symbol Na.

You may wish to use page 8 of the data booklet to help you.

A	B	C
D	E	F

1

(*b*) Identify the **two** elements which react together to form a covalent compound.

You may wish to use page 8 of the data booklet to help you.

A	B	C
D	E	F

1

(*c*) Identify the element used to galvanise iron.

A	B	C
D	E	F

1

(3)

[Turn over

DO NOT WRITE IN THIS MARGIN

Marks | KU | PS

2. A pupil tested the solubility of vitamin C.

The same mass of vitamin C was used in each experiment.

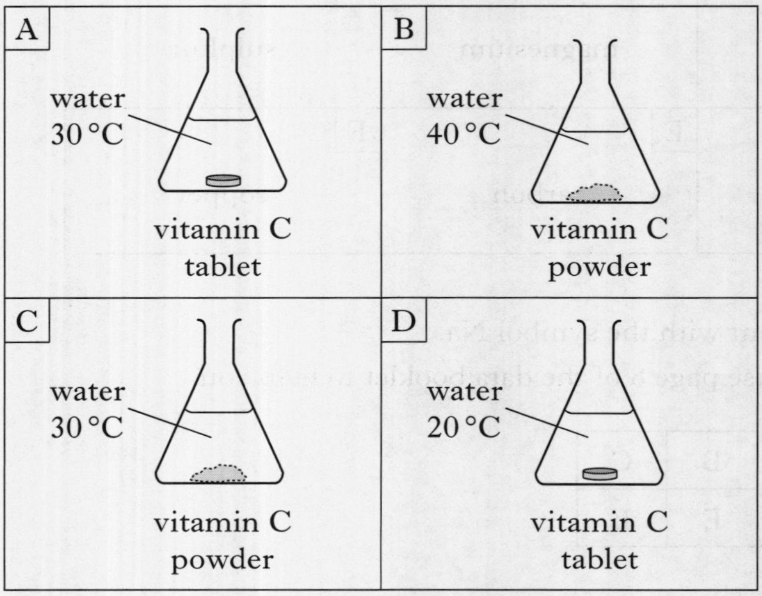

(*a*) Identify the **two** experiments which would be compared to show the effect of particle size on the speed of dissolving.

A	B
C	D

1

(*b*) Identify the experiment in which the vitamin C would take longest to dissolve.

A	B
C	D

1

(2)

DO NOT WRITE IN THIS MARGIN

Marks KU PS

3. The names of some gases are shown in the grid.

A helium	B carbon dioxide	C hydrogen
D nitrogen	E sulphur dioxide	F oxygen

(*a*) Identify the gas **produced** during respiration.

A	B	C
D	E	F

1

(*b*) Identify the gas produced when a carbonate reacts with dilute acid.

A	B	C
D	E	F

1

(*c*) Identify the gas which causes acid rain.

A	B	C
D	E	F

1

(*d*) Identify the **two** gases which react together to form ammonia in the Haber Process.

A	B	C
D	E	F

1

(4)

[Turn over

DO NOT WRITE IN THIS MARGIN

Marks KU PS

4. Various solutions can be used to identify substances.

A iodine solution	B lime water	C ferroxyl indicator
D Benedict's solution	E bromine solution	F pH indicator

(*a*) Identify the solution used to test for $Fe^{2+}(aq)$ ions.

A	B	C
D	E	F

1

(*b*) Identify the solution used to test for glucose.

A	B	C
D	E	F

1

(*c*) Identify the solution used to test for carbon dioxide gas.

A	B	C
D	E	F

1

(3)

Marks KU PS

5. The chart shows the pH of different substances.

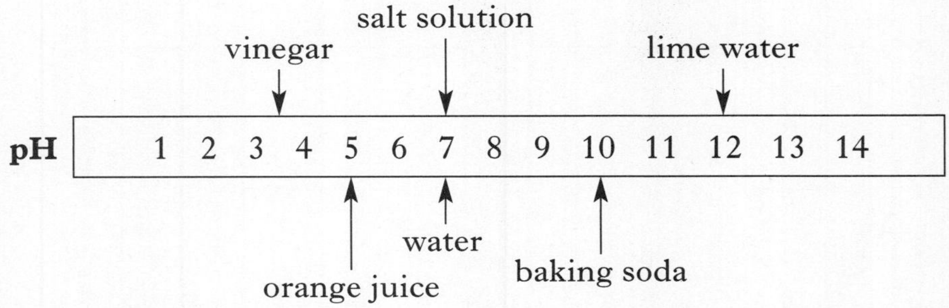

A vinegar	B salt solution	C lime water
D orange juice	E water	F baking soda

(*a*) A wasp sting is alkaline.

Which **two** substances could be used to neutralise a wasp sting?

A	B	C
D	E	F

1

(*b*) Identify the substance which is the most alkaline.

A	B	C
D	E	F

1

(2)

[Turn over

DO NOT WRITE IN THIS MARGIN

Marks | KU | PS

6. Kevin was investigating corrosion.

He set up four experiments as shown in the grid below.

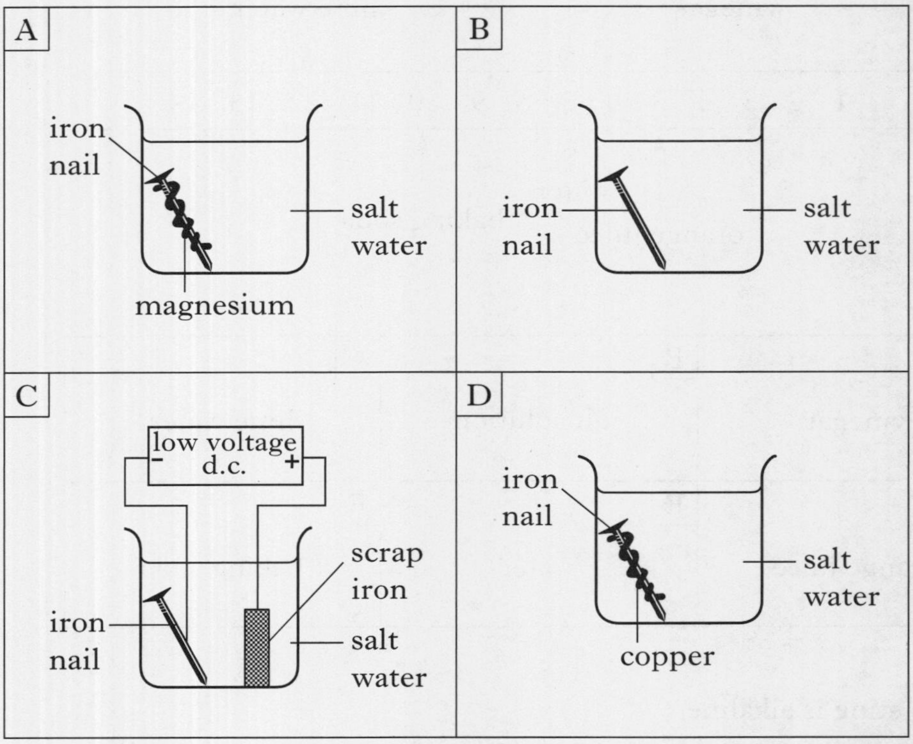

Identify the experiment in which the corrosion of the **nail** was the most rapid.

A	B
C	D

(1)

DO NOT WRITE IN THIS MARGIN

Marks KU PS

7. The names of some hydrocarbons are shown.

A ethene	B propene	C methane
D butane	E hexene	F pentene

(*a*) Identify the hydrocarbon which is the first member of the alkene family.

A	B	C
D	E	F

1

(*b*) Identify the hydrocarbon with **five** carbon atoms in each molecule.

A	B	C
D	E	F

1

(*c*) Identify the hydrocarbon with a boiling point of 30 °C.

You may wish to use page 6 of the data booklet to help you.

A	B	C
D	E	F

1
(3)

[Turn over

DO NOT WRITE IN THIS MARGIN

Marks | KU | PS

8. Gold and silver are both used to make jewellery.

Identify the **two** statements which are true for **both** gold **and** silver.

You may wish to use the data booklet to help you.

A	They are alkali metals.
B	They conduct electricity.
C	They are more reactive than copper.
D	They react with dilute hydrochloric acid.
E	They are found uncombined in the Earth's crust.

A
B
C
D
E

(2)

DO NOT WRITE IN THIS MARGIN

Marks KU PS

PART 2

A total of 40 marks is available in this part of the paper.

9. When manganese dioxide is added to hydrogen peroxide solution, oxygen gas is produced.

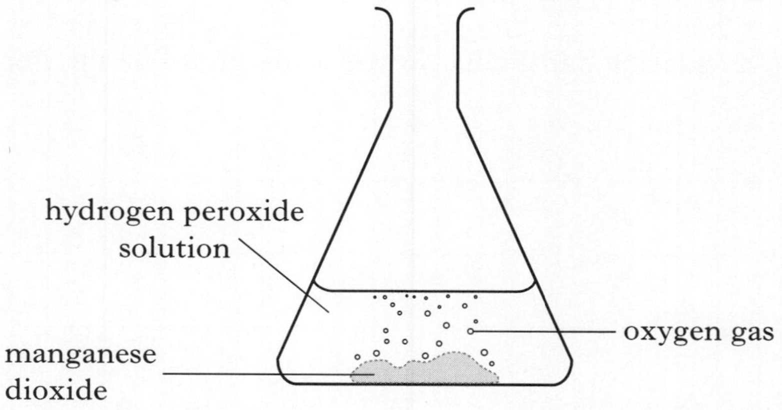

(*a*) Oxygen gas exists as diatomic molecules.

What does **diatomic** mean?

____

____ **1**

(*b*) Heat is produced in the above reaction.

What name is given to a chemical reaction which releases heat?

____ **1**

(*c*) In this reaction manganese dioxide is acting as a catalyst.

What is a catalyst?

____

____

____ **1**

(3)

[Turn over

DO NOT WRITE IN THIS MARGIN

Marks | KU | PS

10. Chlorine and iodine are both members of the same group in the Periodic Table.

(*a*) (i) What is the family name for the group to which chlorine and iodine belong?

_______________ **1**

(ii) Why are chlorine and iodine in the same group of the Periodic Table?

____

____

_______________ **1**

(*b*) The pie chart shows the percentages of iodine used to make other substances.

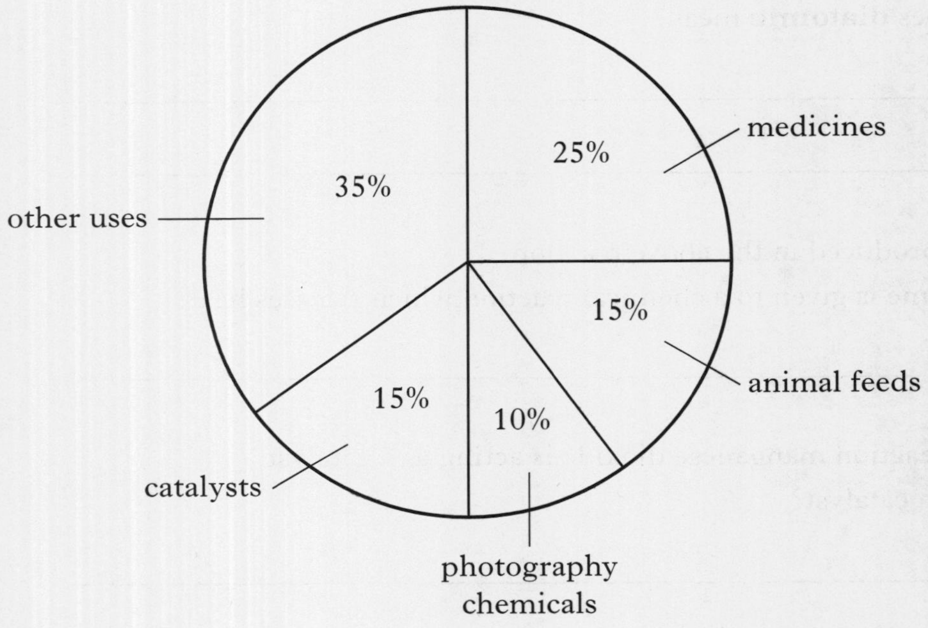

DO NOT WRITE IN THIS MARGIN

Marks KU PS

10. (*b*) (continued)

Present the information as a bar chart.

Use appropriate scales to fill most of the graph paper.

(Additional graph paper, if required, can be found on page 25.)

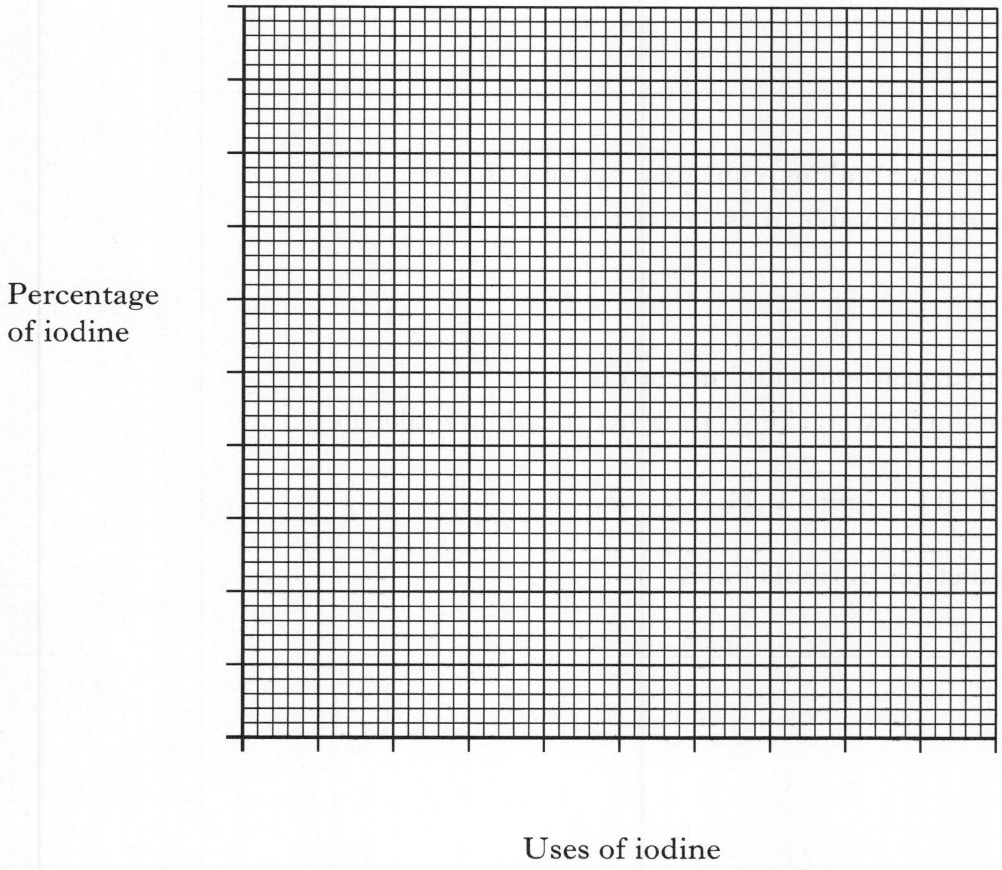

2

(*c*) Calcium iodate is a compound which is added to animal feeds.

Name the elements present in calcium iodate.

______________________________ **1**

(5)

[Turn over

DO NOT WRITE IN THIS MARGIN

Marks | KU | PS

11. Petrol and diesel are mixtures of hydrocarbons which are used as fuels for cars.

(*a*) What is a hydrocarbon?

____

____

____ **1**

(*b*) Diesel has a higher boiling point than petrol.

Which is more flammable, diesel or petrol?

____ **1**

(*c*) Octane is a hydrocarbon found in petrol.

It can be obtained by cracking larger hydrocarbon molecules.

$$C_{18}H_{38} \rightarrow C_8H_{18} + \mathbf{X}$$

Write the molecular formula for **X.**

______________________________ **1**

(3)

DO NOT WRITE IN THIS MARGIN

12. (*a*) A pupil set up the following cell and measured the cell voltage. *Marks* KU PS

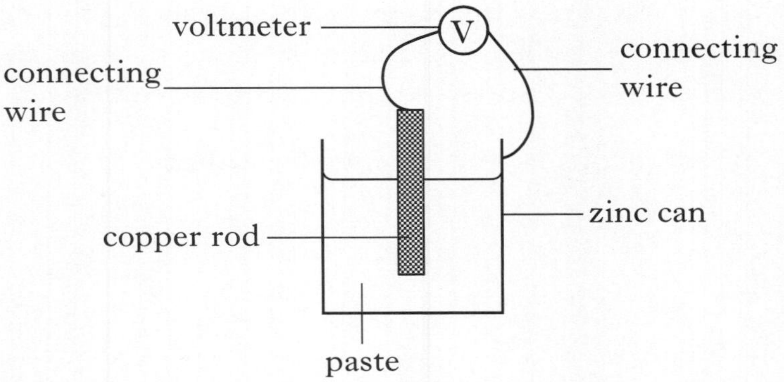

(i) Name the type of charged particle that flows through the connecting wires.

____ 1

(ii) The pupil repeated the experiment using cans made from different metals.

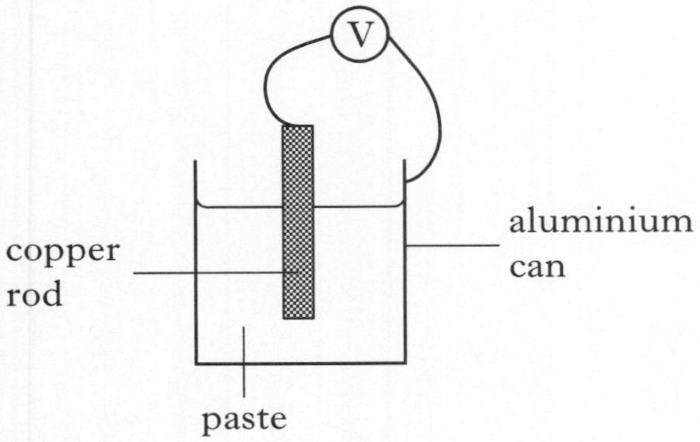

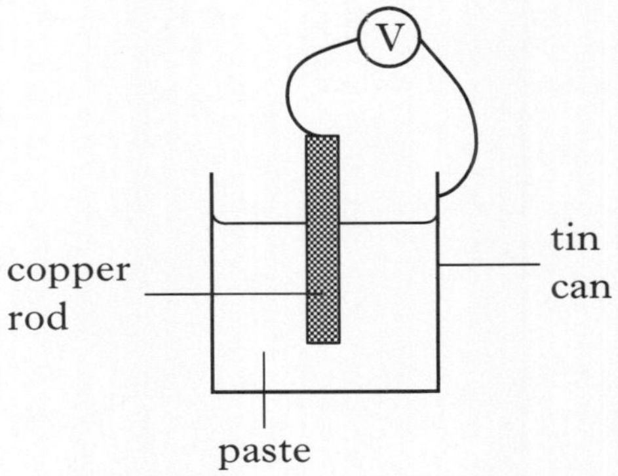

The results are shown in the table.

Metal can	**Cell voltage/V**
aluminium	1·86
zinc	0·92
tin	

Complete the table to show a voltage you might expect for the cell using the tin can.
You may wish to use page 7 of the data booklet to help you. 1

(*b*) A battery is a number of cells joined together.

Give **one** advantage of using a battery rather than mains electricity.

____

____ 1

(3)

DO NOT WRITE IN THIS MARGIN

Marks KU PS

13. Alloys have many uses. Water taps can be made from brass while solder is used to join metal pipes together. Duralumin is used to make the framework for aeroplanes, however cars and ships are made from steel.

(*a*) Present this information in a table with suitable headings. **2**

(*b*) Solder is an alloy of tin and lead only.

The melting point of solder depends on the percentages of tin and lead mixed together.

Percentage of tin	**Melting point of solder/°C**
25	270
45	225
65	180
85	205

DO NOT WRITE IN THIS MARGIN

Marks KU PS

13. (*b*) (continued)

(i) What percentages of **tin** and **lead** are present in the solder with the **lowest** melting point?

Tin _______ %

Lead ______ % **1**

(ii) Solder is used in electronic circuit boards.

Apart from its low melting point, what other property of solder makes it suitable for use in electronic circuit boards?

____

____

____ **1**

(4)

[Turn over

DO NOT WRITE IN THIS MARGIN

Marks KU PS

14. Butene has the structural formula shown below.

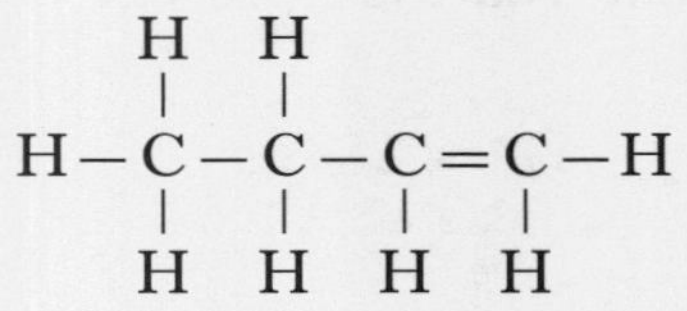

(*a*) Butene reacts with hydrogen gas.

(i) Name the type of chemical reaction which takes place when butene reacts with hydrogen gas, H_2.

______________________________ **1**

(ii) Write the molecular formula for the product of the reaction.

______________________________ **1**

(*b*) Butene can be converted into a polymer.

(i) Name the polymer made from butene.

______________________________ **1**

(ii) The polymer is **non**-biodegradable.
Suggest why this may be an advantage.

____

____

______________________________ **1**

(4)

DO NOT WRITE IN THIS MARGIN

Marks | KU | PS

15. The following apparatus can be used to electrolyse molten sodium chloride in industry.

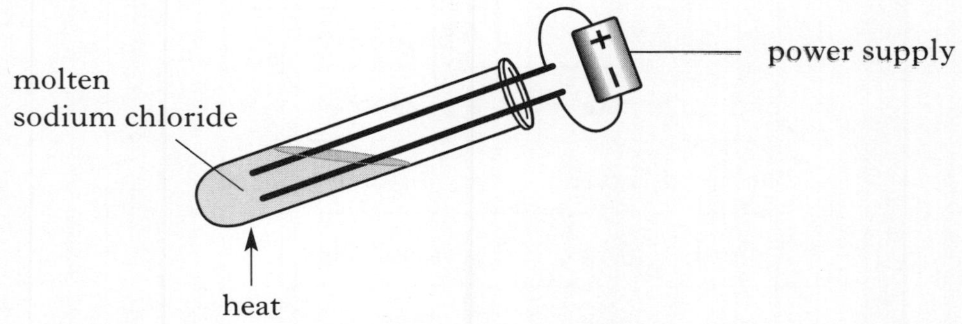

(*a*) State what is meant by electrolysis.

____

____

____ **1**

(*b*) Why do ionic compounds, like sodium chloride, conduct electricity when molten?

____

____ **1**

(*c*) Name the product formed at the positive electrode.

____ **1**

(*d*) A small amount of calcium chloride was added to lower the melting point of the sodium chloride.

Suggest why this would be an advantage in industry.

____

____ **1**

(4)

[Turn over

DO NOT WRITE IN THIS MARGIN

Marks | KU | PS

16. Information about the solubility of some barium salts in water is given in the table.

Salt	Solubility
barium nitrate	soluble
barium chloride	soluble
barium sulphate	insoluble
barium carbonate	insoluble

(*a*) A "barium meal" is given to some patients before taking an X-ray of their stomach. A barium meal contains barium sulphate which is poisonous.

(i) Suggest a reason why the "barium meal" does not poison the patient.

____

____

____ **1**

(ii) The stomach produces dilute hydrochloric acid to help digestion. Suggest why barium carbonate is **not** used in a "barium meal".

____

____

____ **1**

(*b*) Write the formula for barium carbonate.

____ **1**

(3)

DO NOT WRITE IN THIS MARGIN

Marks KU PS

17. Ethylene glycol has the formula $C_2H_6O_2$.

(*a*) Name the **two** products formed when ethylene glycol is burned completely in oxygen.

____ **1**

(*b*) Ethylene glycol is used to make polyesters. Polyesters are thermoplastic.
What does **thermoplastic** mean?

____

____ **1**

(*c*) Ethylene glycol is also used as antifreeze in car radiators. Salt could be used as antifreeze instead of ethylene glycol.
Suggest why salt is **not** used as antifreeze in steel radiators.

____

____ **1**

(3)

[Turn over

DO NOT WRITE IN THIS MARGIN

Marks KU PS

18. During photosynthesis green plants produce oxygen.

(*a*) Name the substance in green plants which absorbs light during photosynthesis.

______________________________ **1**

(*b*) A pupil set up the apparatus shown to investigate the rate of photosynthesis. Oxygen gas produced by the plant was collected in the test tube.

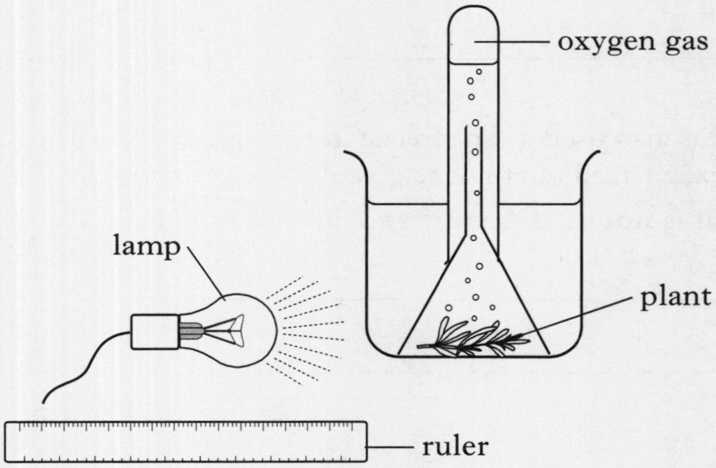

Distance of lamp from plant/cm	Number of bubbles of oxygen gas produced in one minute
30	24
40	19
60	10
100	4

(i) What effect does the distance of the lamp from the plant have on the number of bubbles of oxygen gas produced?

____

____

______________________________ **1**

DO NOT WRITE IN THIS MARGIN

Marks KU PS

18. (*b*) (continued)

(ii) Give **one** factor that needs to be kept the same to make this experiment fair.

____ **1**

(*c*) During photosynthesis glucose is also produced.

Name the process used to convert glucose to alcohol.

____ **1**

(4)

[Turn over

DO NOT WRITE IN THIS MARGIN

Marks | KU | PS

19. Ammonia gas can be prepared in the laboratory by heating a mixture of ammonium chloride and calcium hydroxide.

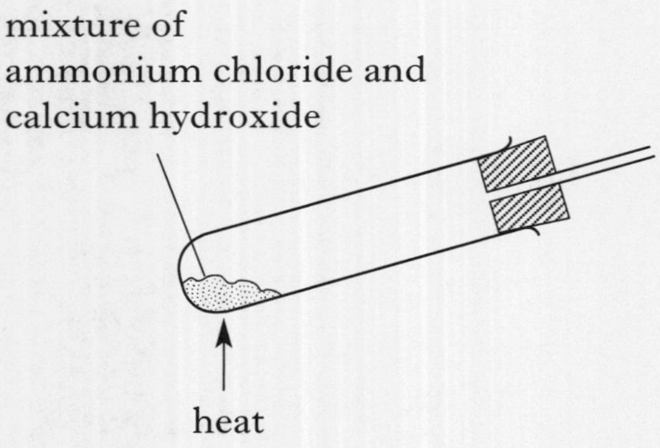

(*a*) Ammonia gas is soluble in water and is lighter than air.

Complete the diagram to show how a sample of ammonia gas could be collected.

(An additional diagram, if required, can be found on page 26.) **1**

(*b*) Describe a chemical test to show the presence of ammonia gas.

____

______________________________ **1**

(*c*) Ammonia can be used to make ammonium nitrate fertiliser.

(i) Name the essential element which plants obtain from ammonium nitrate.

______________________________ **1**

(ii) Over the last 100 years there has been an increase in the demand for fertilisers.

Why is this?

____

____

______________________________ **1**

(4)

[*END OF QUESTION PAPER*]

DO NOT WRITE IN THIS MARGIN

KU PS

ADDITIONAL SPACE FOR ANSWERS

ADDITIONAL GRAPH PAPER FOR QUESTION 10(*b*)

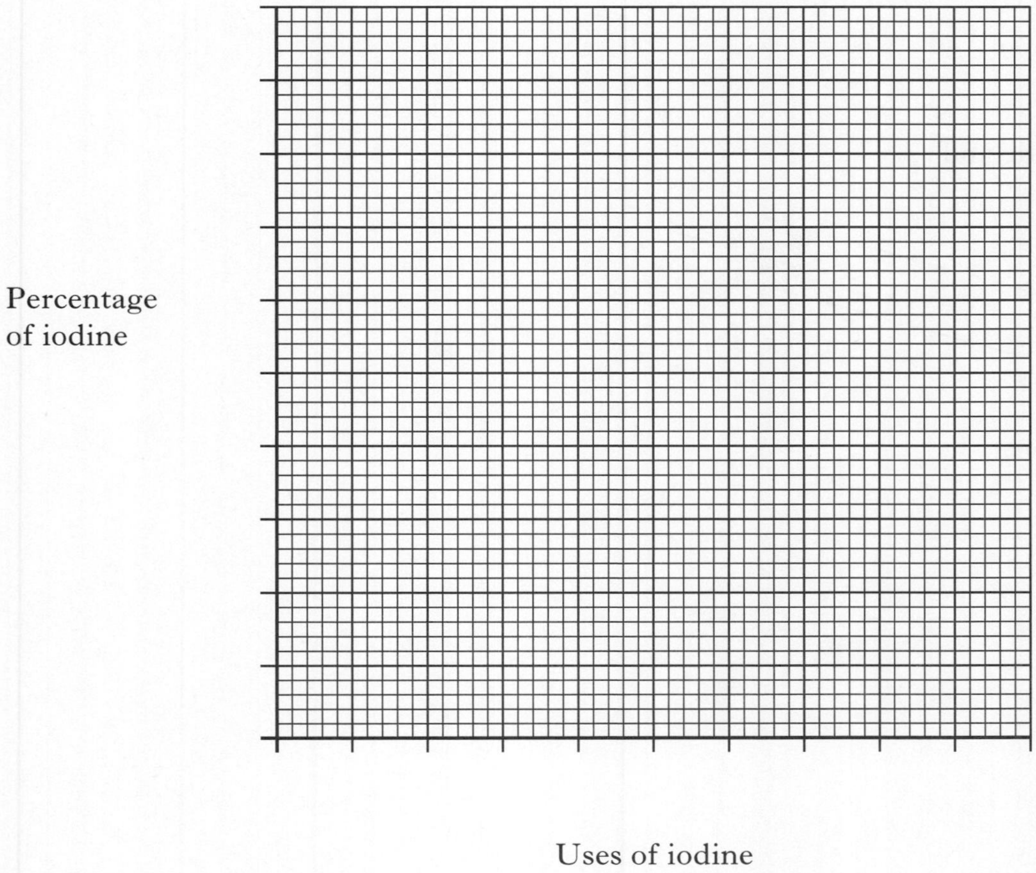

DO NOT WRITE IN THIS MARGIN

KU	PS

ADDITIONAL SPACE FOR ANSWERS

ADDITIONAL DIAGRAM FOR QUESTION 19(*a*)

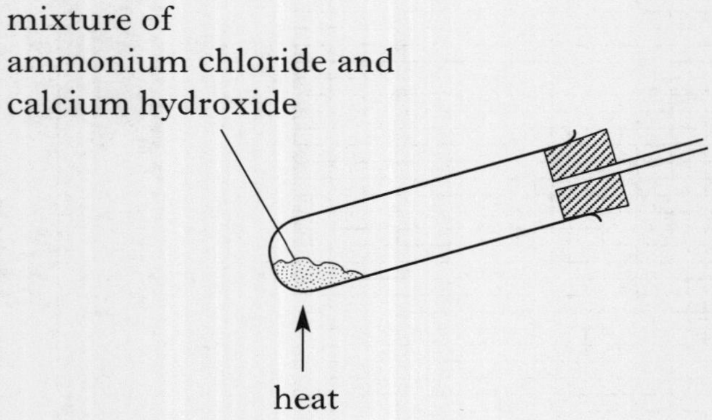

DO NOT WRITE IN THIS MARGIN

KU	PS

ADDITIONAL SPACE FOR ANSWERS

DO NOT WRITE IN THIS MARGIN

KU	PS

ADDITIONAL SPACE FOR ANSWERS

2006 | General

[BLANK PAGE]

FOR OFFICIAL USE

G

	KU	PS
Total Marks		

0500/401

NATIONAL QUALIFICATIONS 2006

MONDAY, 8 MAY
9.00 AM – 10.30 AM

CHEMISTRY
STANDARD GRADE
General Level

Fill in these boxes and read what is printed below.

Full name of centre

Town

Forename(s)

Surname

Date of birth
Day Month Year

Scottish candidate number

Number of seat

1 All questions should be attempted.

2 Necessary data will be found in the Data Booklet provided for Chemistry at Standard Grade and Intermediate 2.

3 The questions may be answered in any order but all answers are to be written in this answer book, and must be written clearly and legibly in ink.

4 Rough work, if any should be necessary, as well as the fair copy, is to be written in this book.

Rough work should be scored through when the fair copy has been written.

5 Additional space for answers and rough work will be found at the end of the book.

6 The size of the space provided for an answer should not be taken as an indication of how much to write. It is not necessary to use all the space.

7 Before leaving the examination room you must give this book to the invigilator. If you do not, you may lose all the marks for this paper.

SCOTTISH QUALIFICATIONS AUTHORITY

PART 1

In Questions 1 to 8 of this part of the paper, an answer is given by circling the appropriate letter (or letters) in the answer grid provided.

In some questions, two letters are required for full marks.

If more than the correct number of answers is given, marks will be deducted.

A total of 20 marks is available in this part of the paper.

SAMPLE QUESTION

A CH_4	B H_2	C CO_2
D CO	E C_2H_5OH	F C

(*a*) Identify the hydrocarbon.

A	B	C
D	E	F

The one correct answer to part (*a*) is A. This should be circled.

(*b*) Identify the **two** elements.

A	B	C
D	E	F

As indicated in this question, there are **two** correct answers to part (*b*). These are B and F. Both answers are circled.

If, after you have recorded your answer, you decide that you have made an error and wish to make a change, you should cancel the original answer and circle the answer you now consider to be correct. Thus, in part (*a*), if you want to change an answer A to an answer D, your answer sheet would look like this:

A	B	C
D	E	F

If you want to change back to an answer which has already been scored out, you should enter a tick (✓) in the box of the answer of your choice, thus:

✓ A	B	C
D	E	F

DO NOT WRITE IN THIS MARGIN

Marks | KU | PS

1. The grid contains the names of some metals.

A potassium	B gold	C magnesium
D copper	E zinc	F calcium

(*a*) Identify the metal which has the symbol, K.
You may wish to use page 8 of the data booklet to help you.

A	B	C
D	E	F

1

(*b*) Identify the metal which was discovered in the year 1775.
You may wish to use page 8 of the data booklet to help you.

A	B	C
D	E	F

1

(*c*) Identify the metal which is used to galvanise iron.

A	B	C
D	E	F

1

(*d*) Identify the metal which gives an orange-red flame colour.
You may wish to use page 4 of the data booklet to help you.

A	B	C
D	E	F

1
(4)

[Turn over

Marks KU PS

2. Lesley and Scott studied the reaction of magnesium with dilute acid.

The same mass of magnesium was used in each experiment.

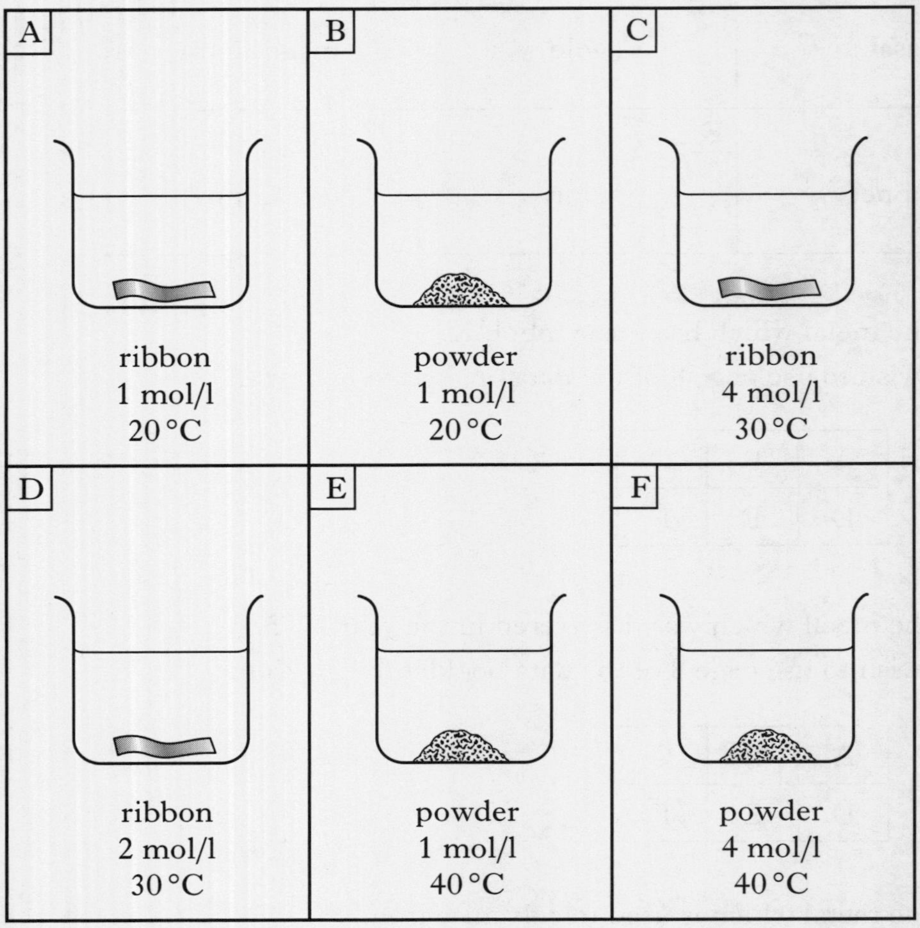

Identify the **two** experiments which could be used to show the effect of temperature on the rate of the reaction.

A	B	C
D	E	F

(1)

DO NOT WRITE IN THIS MARGIN

Marks KU PS

3. Hydrocarbons contain hydrogen and carbon only.

A butene	B methane	C hexene
D pentane	E pentene	F propene

(*a*) Identify the **two** hydrocarbons which are alkanes.

A	B	C
D	E	F

1

(*b*) Identify the hydrocarbon which could be produced when ethane is cracked.

A	B	C
D	E	F

1

(*c*) Identify the hydrocarbon with the highest boiling point.

You may wish to use page 6 of the data booklet to help you.

A	B	C
D	E	F

1

(3)

[Turn over

DO NOT WRITE IN THIS MARGIN

Marks KU PS

4. Class 4A made some statements about the effect of adding water to an alkaline solution.

A	The pH of the solution will rise.
B	The solution will become more concentrated.
C	The pH of the solution will fall towards 7.
D	Adding water will have no effect on the solution.

Identify the correct statement.

A
B
C
D

(1)

DO NOT WRITE IN THIS MARGIN

Marks KU PS

5. Electricity can be produced using electrochemical cells.

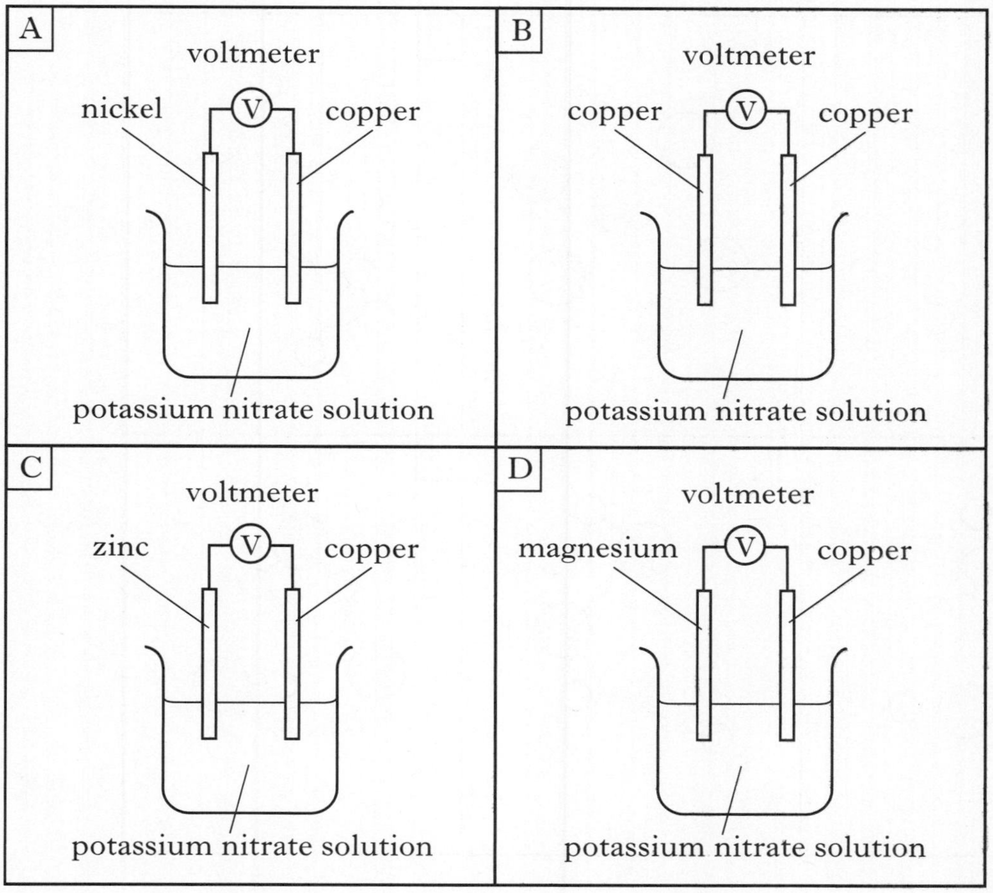

(*a*) Identify the arrangement which would **not** produce electricity.

A	B
C	D

1

(*b*) Identify the arrangement which would produce the greatest voltage.
You may wish to use page 7 of the data booklet to help you.

A	B
C	D

1

(2)

[Turn over

DO NOT WRITE IN THIS MARGIN

Marks KU PS

6. Many substances can be represented by simple diagrams.

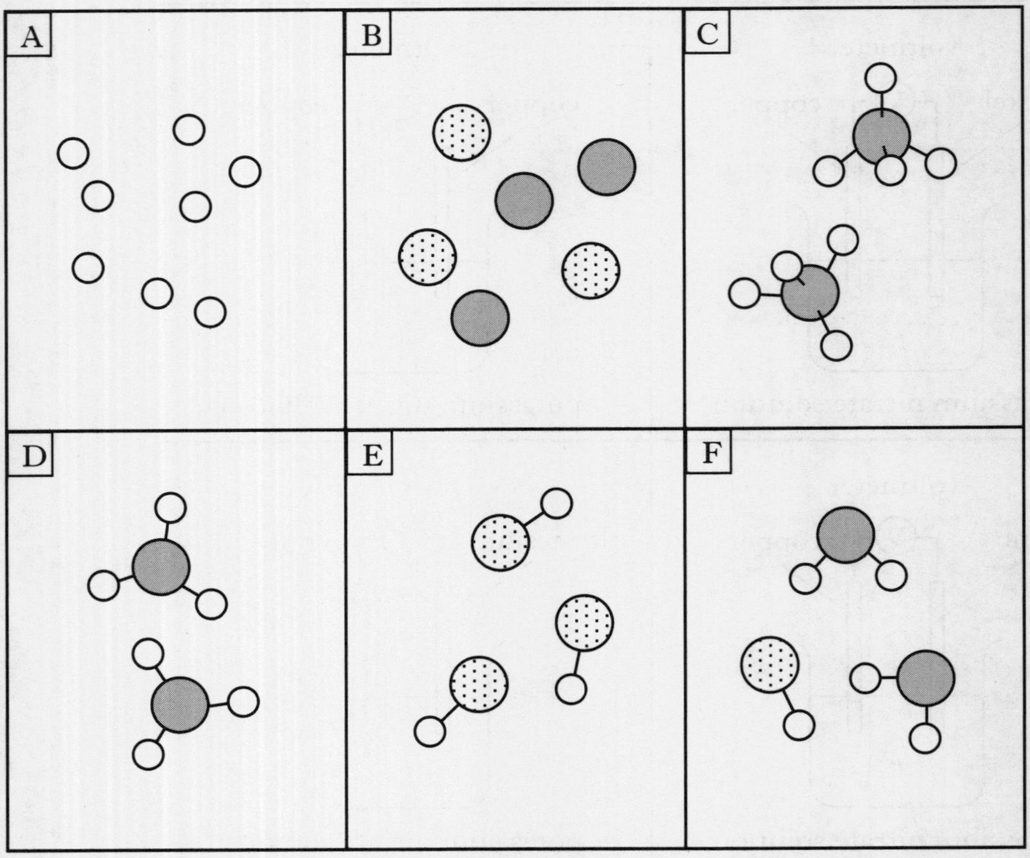

(*a*) Identify the diagram which could represent an element.

A	B	C
D	E	F

1

(*b*) Identify the diagram which contains **diatomic** molecules.

A	B	C
D	E	F

1

(*c*) Identify the **two** diagrams which **do not** contain molecules.

A	B	C
D	E	F

1

(3)

DO NOT WRITE IN THIS MARGIN

Marks KU PS

7. The grid contains the names of some chemical processes.

A respiration	B fermentation	C filtration
D photosynthesis	E distillation	F cracking

(a) Identify the process used to separate alcohol from water.

A	B	C
D	E	F

1

(b) Identify the process in which chlorophyll absorbs light energy.

A	B	C
D	E	F

1

(c) Identify the **two** processes in which carbon dioxide is produced.

A	B	C
D	E	F

2

(4)

[Turn over

DO NOT WRITE IN THIS MARGIN

Marks KU PS

8. Stephen was investigating electrical conductivity.

He set up four experiments.

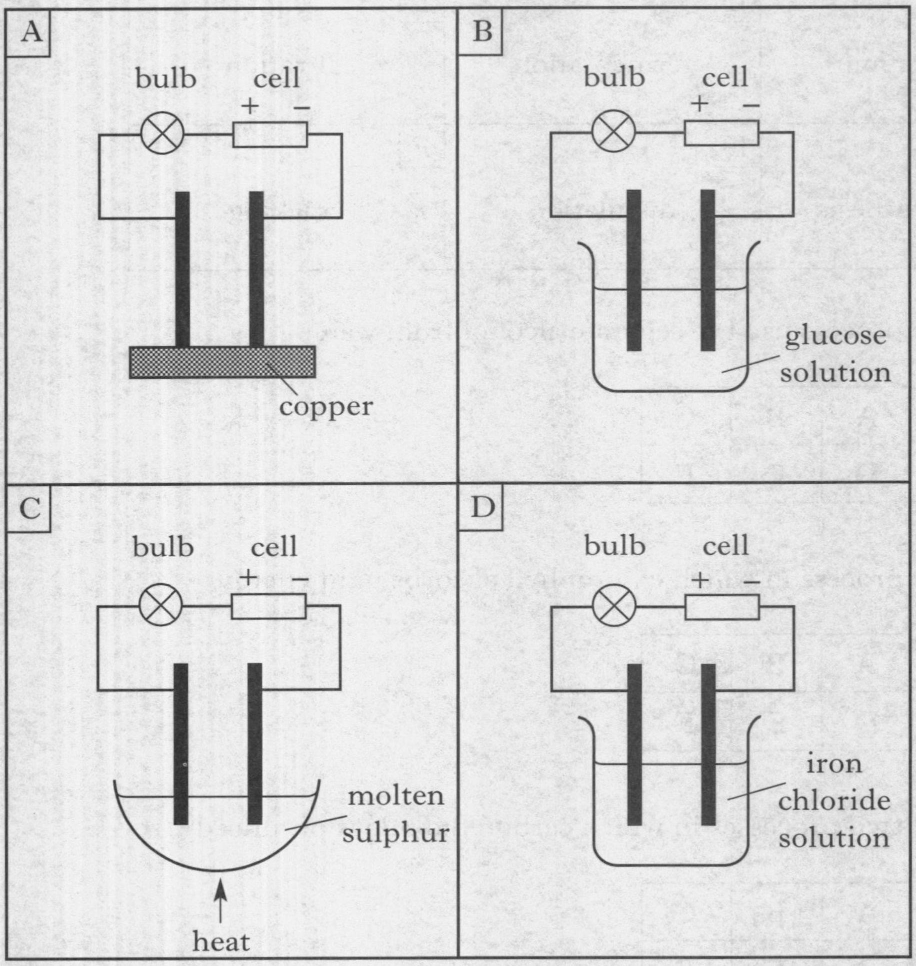

Identify the **two** experiments in which the bulb will light.

A	B
C	D

(2)

DO NOT WRITE IN THIS MARGIN

Marks KU PS

PART 2

A total of 40 marks is available in this part of the paper.

9. When water is added to some types of Vitamin C tablets, carbon dioxide gas is produced.

A student set up the following experiment and timed how long it took for the gas produced to blow off the container lid.

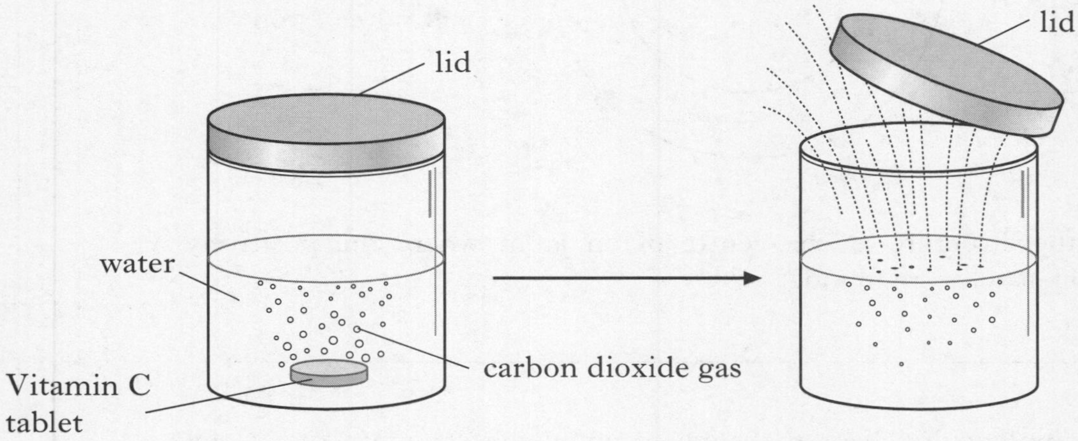

(*a*) State the test for carbon dioxide.

____ **1**

(*b*) The student repeated the experiment using the same volume of water and the same mass of a **crushed** Vitamin C tablet.

What effect would this have on the time taken for the lid to be blown off the container?

____ **1**

(*c*) The diagram shows a molecule of Vitamin C.

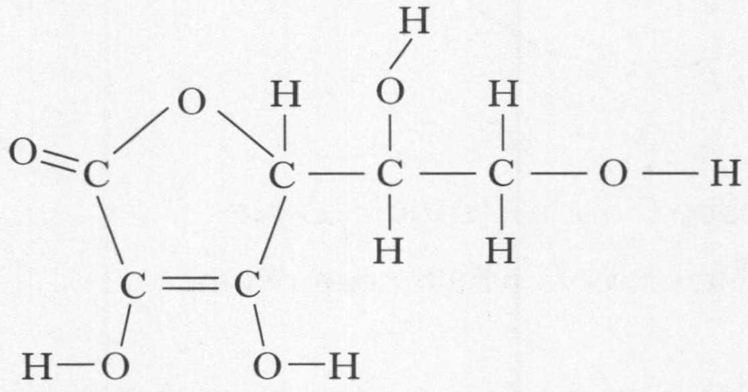

Complete the formula to show the number of each type of atom in this molecule.

C H O **1**

(3)

DO NOT WRITE IN THIS MARGIN

Marks | KU | PS

10. An atom can be represented by a simple diagram.

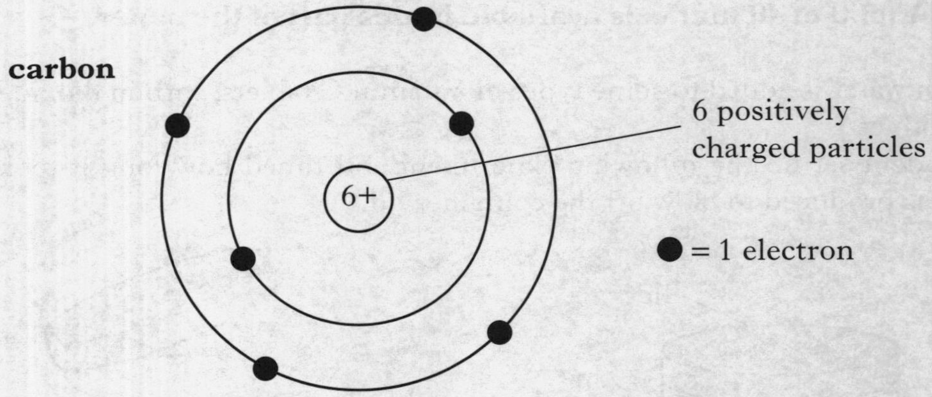

(*a*) Name the structure at the centre of an atom where the positively charged particles are found.

______________________________ **1**

(*b*) (i) Complete the diagram below to show the structure of a neon atom.

You may wish to use page 1 of the data booklet to help you.

(An additional diagram, if required, can be found on page 23.)

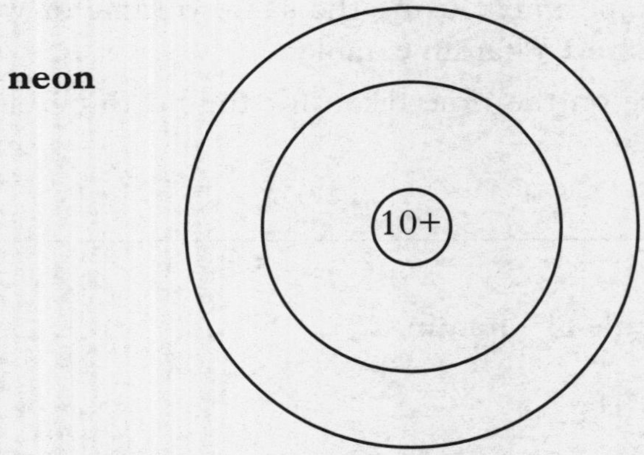

1

(ii) Neon is found in Group 0 of the Periodic Table.

Name the family of elements to which neon belongs.

______________________________ **1**

(3)

DO NOT WRITE IN THIS MARGIN

Marks | KU | PS

11. Crude oil and natural gas are fossil fuels.

(*a*) Fossil fuels are a finite resource.

What is meant by the term **finite**?

______________________________ **1**

(*b*) (i) Describe how crude oil was formed.

____

____

____

______________________________ **2**

(ii) The diagram shows fractional distillation of crude oil.

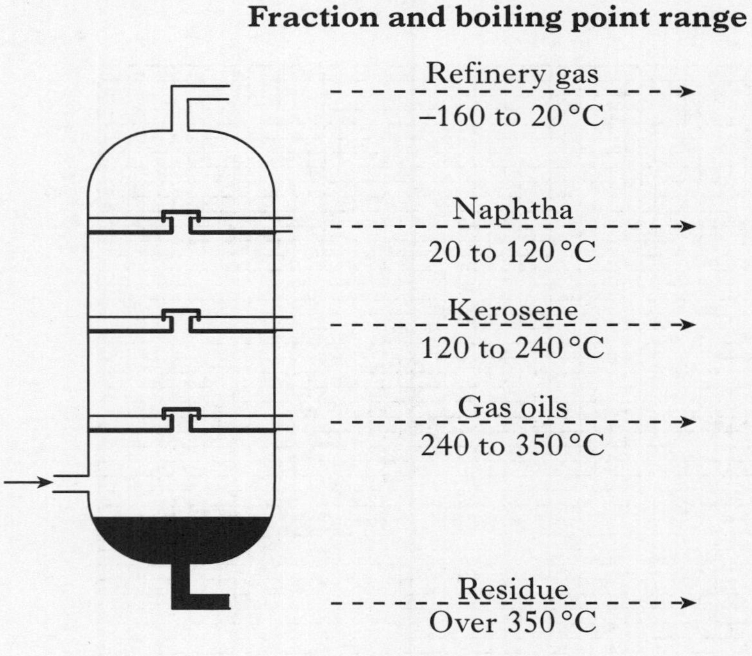

Name the fraction which can be used to produce tar for roads.

______________________________ **1**

(*c*) Some sources of natural gas contain sulphur compounds.

Why are the sulphur compounds removed before the natural gas is used as a fuel?

____

______________________________ **1**

(5)

DO NOT WRITE IN THIS MARGIN

Marks KU PS

12. Nitrates are chemicals found in some foods.
The table shows the sources of nitrates in our diet.

Source of nitrates	%
green vegetables	45
water	20
milk	15
potatoes	10
other foods	10

(*a*) Draw a bar graph to show the information in the table.
Use appropriate scales to fill most of the graph paper.
(Additional graph paper, if required, can be found on page 23.)

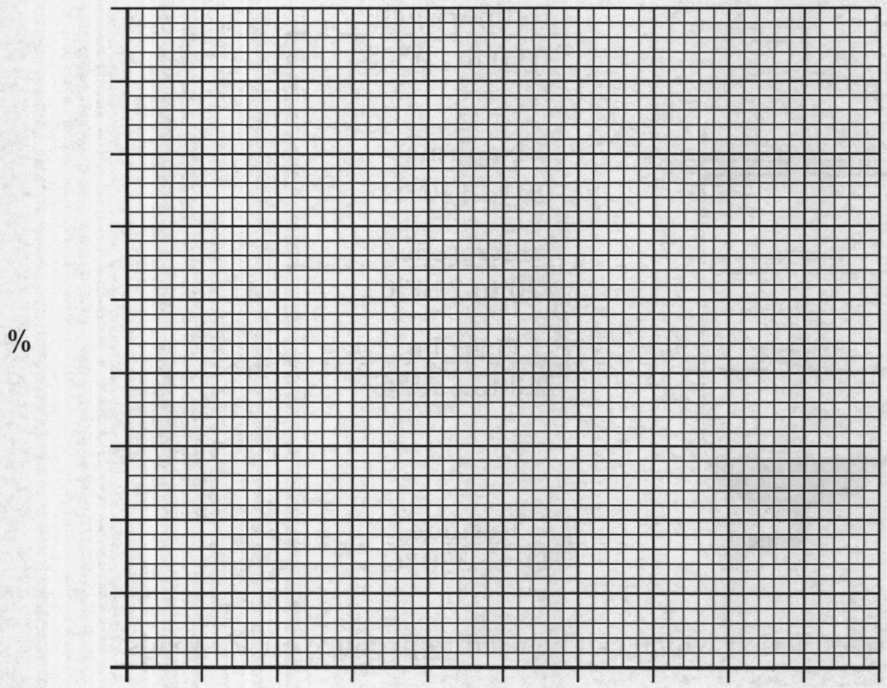

2

DO NOT WRITE IN THIS MARGIN

12. (continued) *Marks* KU PS

(*b*) Nitrates are used as fertilisers as they contain the essential element nitrogen.

(i) Name **one** other essential element for plant growth.

____ **1**

(ii) Suggest another property of nitrates which makes them suitable for use as fertilisers.

____ **1**

(*c*) Certain types of plants contain bacteria which can convert nitrogen from the air into nitrogen compounds.

Which part of the plant contains these bacteria?

____ **1**

(5)

[Turn over

DO NOT WRITE IN THIS MARGIN

Marks | KU | PS

13. (*a*) Name the elements present in lead nitrate.

____ **1**

(*b*) When lead nitrate solution and potassium iodide solution are mixed, a chemical reaction takes place.

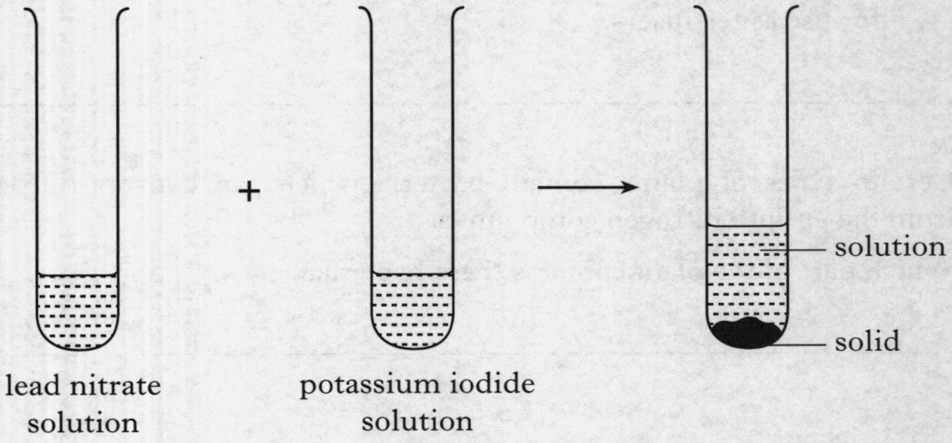

(i) Name the solid formed in this reaction.

You may wish to use page 5 of the data booklet to help you.

____ **1**

(ii) How could a sample of the solid be separated from the solution?

____

____

____ **1**

(3)

DO NOT WRITE IN THIS MARGIN

Marks KU PS

14. The table contains information about the reaction of butene with some of the Group 7 elements.

Element	Speed of reaction
fluorine	explosive
chlorine	very fast
bromine	fast

(*a*) Predict the speed of the reaction when butene reacts with iodine.

____ **1**

(*b*) Butene is an unsaturated hydrocarbon.

(i) Write the molecular formula for butene.

____ **1**

(ii) Describe a chemical test, including the result, to show that butene is unsaturated.

____

____ **1**

(3)

[Turn over

DO NOT WRITE IN THIS MARGIN

Marks | KU | PS

15. The elements found in Group 0 have many uses.

Helium is lighter than air and can be used in airships. Neon is used in advertising signs and the main use of argon is in light bulbs. Krypton can be used in certain types of lasers.

(*a*) Present this information as a table with suitable headings. **2**

(*b*) Information on Group 0 elements is shown below.

Atomic number	2	10	18	36	54
Atomic size (nm)	0·49	0·51	0·88	1·03	1·24

What happens to the atomic size as the atomic number increases?

____

____ **1**

(*c*) Hydrogen is another gas which is lighter than air and in the past was used in airships.

Suggest why hydrogen is no longer used in airships.

____ **1**

(4)

DO NOT WRITE IN THIS MARGIN

Marks KU PS

16. **A method of making sulphuric acid**

Ammonia reacts with **oxygen** to produce **nitrogen monoxide**. **Water** is also produced in the reaction. The **nitrogen monoxide** reacts with more **oxygen** to form **nitrogen dioxide**. **Sulphuric acid** is produced when the **nitrogen dioxide** reacts with **sulphurous acid**.

(*a*) Use this information to complete the flow diagram.

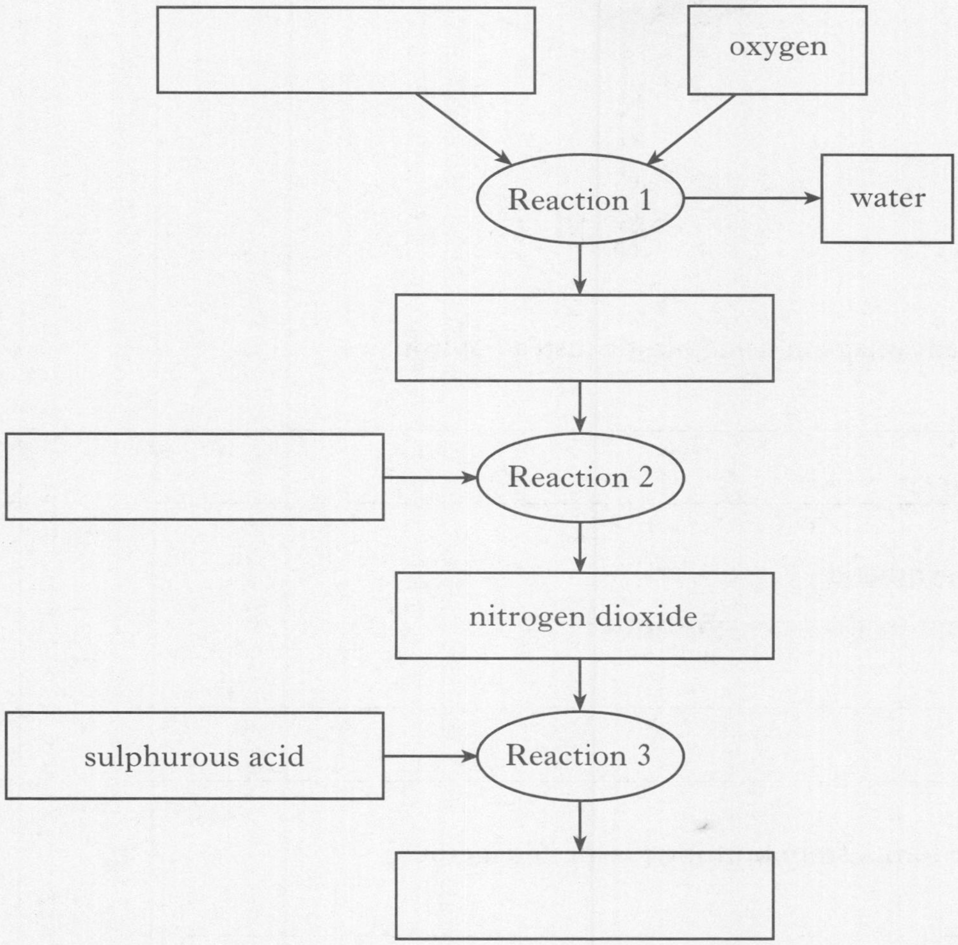

2

(*b*) Write the formula for nitrogen dioxide.

____________________________ 1

(3)

[Turn over

DO NOT WRITE IN THIS MARGIN

Marks | KU | PS

17. Guttering is used on the outside of houses to collect rain water and drain it away from the roof. Guttering can be made from plastic or iron.

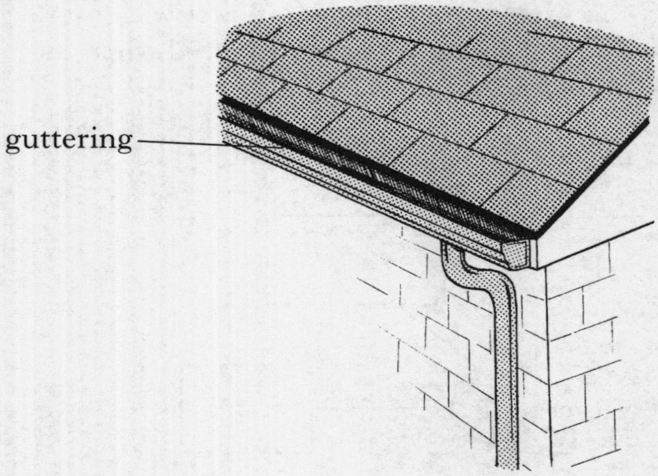

(*a*) Suggest an advantage in using plastic instead of iron.

____

____ **1**

(*b*) Plastics are synthetic.

What is meant by the term **synthetic**?

____

____ **1**

(*c*) Why are the fumes from burning plastics dangerous?

____

____ **1**

(3)

DO NOT WRITE IN THIS MARGIN

Marks KU PS

18. Michael set up the following experiments.

He tested nitric acid solutions of different concentrations.

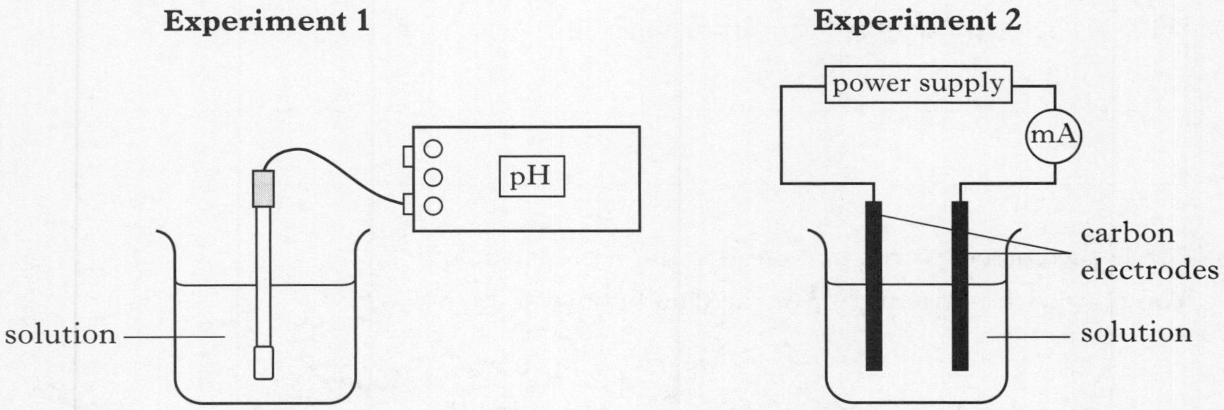

His results are shown in the table.

Nitric acid solution	pH	Current/mA
A	1	380
B	2	120
C	3	20

(*a*) Which nitric acid solution is the most acidic, **A**, **B** or **C**?

______________ **1**

(*b*) Predict the current, in mA, for a nitric acid solution of pH4.

______________ **1**

(*c*) Suggest a factor that Michael should have kept constant in **Experiment 2** to make a fair comparison.

______________________________ **1**

(3)

[Turn over

DO NOT WRITE IN THIS MARGIN

Marks | KU | PS

19. Maggie was advised not to wear a silver ring and a gold ring on the same finger. The sweat from her hand would act as an electrolyte and a cell would be set up.

(*a*) What is the purpose of an electrolyte in a cell?

____

____ **1**

(*b*) Circle the correct words to complete the sentence below.

You may wish to use page 7 of the data booklet to help you.

In the cell, electrons flow from the {gold / silver} ring to the {gold / silver} ring. **1**

(*c*) 18-carat gold is a mixture of gold with other metals.

(i) What name is given to a mixture of metals such as 18-carat gold?

____________________________ **1**

(ii) 18-carat gold contains 75% gold and 5% silver. The rest is copper.

Label the pie chart to show the name and percentage of each metal used to make 18-carat gold.

(An additional pie chart, if required, can be found on page 24.)

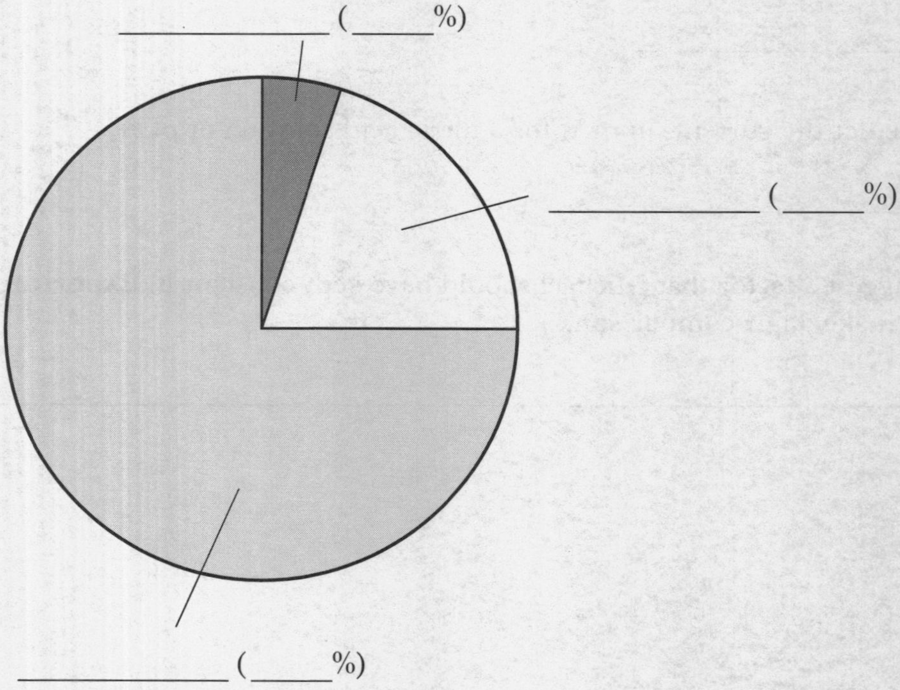

2

(5)

[*END OF QUESTION PAPER*]

DO NOT WRITE IN THIS MARGIN

KU	PS

ADDITIONAL SPACE FOR ANSWERS

ADDITIONAL DIAGRAM FOR QUESTION 10(*b*)(i)

neon

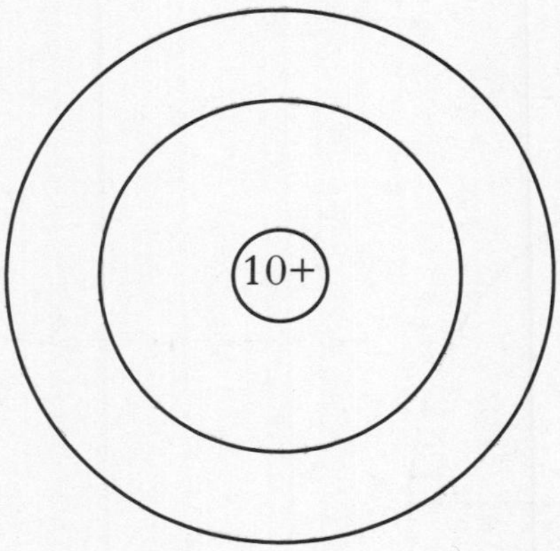

ADDITIONAL GRAPH PAPER FOR QUESTION 12(*a*)

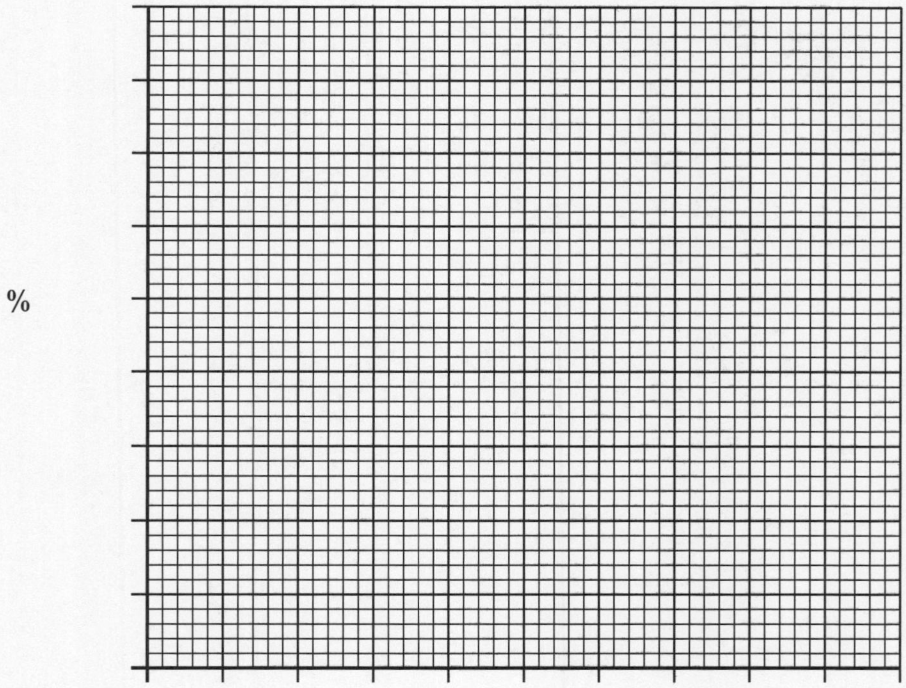

DO NOT WRITE IN THIS MARGIN

KU	PS

ADDITIONAL SPACE FOR ANSWERS

ADDITIONAL PIE CHART FOR QUESTION 19(*c*)(ii)

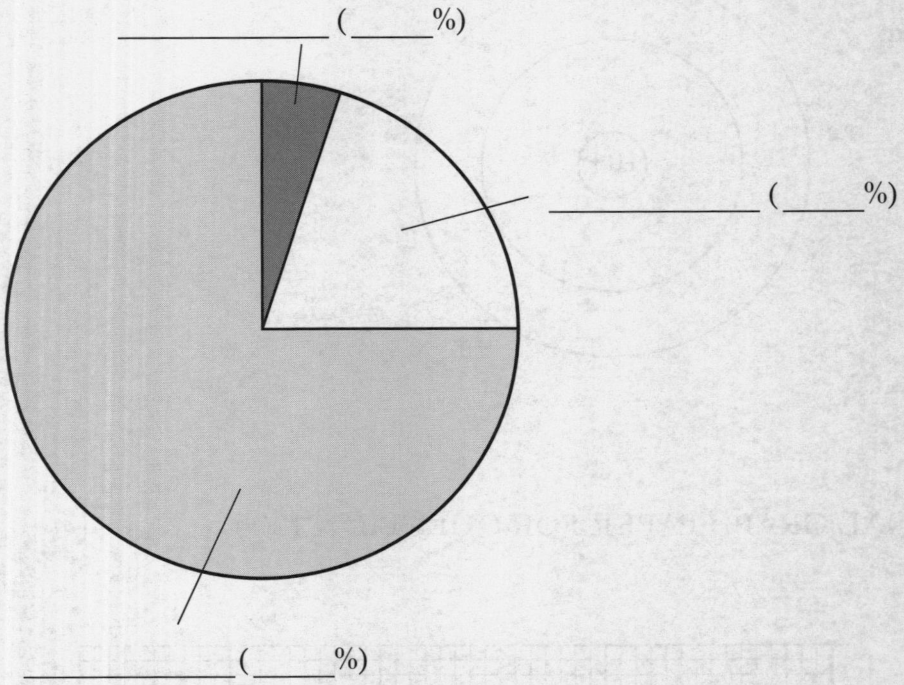

2007 | General

[BLANK PAGE]

FOR OFFICIAL USE

G

	KU	PS
Total Marks		

0500/401

NATIONAL QUALIFICATIONS 2007

THURSDAY, 10 MAY
9.00 AM – 10.30 AM

CHEMISTRY
STANDARD GRADE
General Level

Fill in these boxes and read what is printed below.

Full name of centre

Town

Forename(s)

Surname

Date of birth
Day Month Year

Scottish candidate number

Number of seat

1 All questions should be attempted.

2 Necessary data will be found in the Data Booklet provided for Chemistry at Standard Grade and Intermediate 2.

3 The questions may be answered in any order but all answers are to be written in this answer book, and must be written clearly and legibly in ink.

4 Rough work, if any should be necessary, as well as the fair copy, is to be written in this book.

Rough work should be scored through when the fair copy has been written.

5 Additional space for answers and rough work will be found at the end of the book.

6 The size of the space provided for an answer should not be taken as an indication of how much to write. It is not necessary to use all the space.

7 Before leaving the examination room you must give this book to the invigilator. If you do not, you may lose all the marks for this paper.

SCOTTISH QUALIFICATIONS AUTHORITY

PART 1

In Questions 1 to 8 of this part of the paper, an answer is given by circling the appropriate letter (or letters) in the answer grid provided.

In some questions, two letters are required for full marks.

If more than the correct number of answers is given, marks will be deducted.

A total of 20 marks is available in this part of the paper.

SAMPLE QUESTION

A CH_4	B H_2	C CO_2
D CO	E C_2H_5OH	F C

(*a*) Identify the hydrocarbon.

(A)	B	C
D	E	F

The one correct answer to part (*a*) is A. This should be circled.

(*b*) Identify the **two** elements.

A	(B)	C
D	E	(F)

As indicated in this question, there are **two** correct answers to part (*b*). These are B and F. Both answers are circled.

If, after you have recorded your answer, you decide that you have made an error and wish to make a change, you should cancel the original answer and circle the answer you now consider to be correct. Thus, in part (*a*), if you want to change an answer A to an answer D, your answer sheet would look like this:

~~(A)~~	B	C
(D)	E	F

If you want to change back to an answer which has already been scored out, you should enter a tick (✓) in the box of the answer of your choice, thus:

✓ ~~(A)~~	B	C
~~(D)~~	E	F

DO NOT WRITE IN THIS MARGIN

Marks KU PS

1. The grid contains the names of some elements.

A copper	B magnesium	C iron
D nitrogen	E potassium	F fluorine

(*a*) Identify the element discovered in 1807.

You may wish to use page 8 of the data booklet to help you.

A	B	C
D	E	F

1

(*b*) Identify the element found in the same group as calcium.

You may wish to use page 8 of the data booklet to help you.

A	B	C
D	E	F

1

(*c*) Identify the **two** elements which combine to form a covalent compound.

A	B	C
D	E	F

1

(3)

[Turn over

DO NOT WRITE IN THIS MARGIN

Marks | KU | PS

2. The grid shows the names of some metals.

A lithium	B gold	C iron
D zinc	E calcium	F magnesium

(*a*) Identify the metal found uncombined in the Earth's crust.

A	B	C
D	E	F

1

(*b*) Identify the metal produced in a blast furnace.

A	B	C
D	E	F

1

(*c*) Identify the metal used as the catalyst in the Haber process.

A	B	C
D	E	F

1

(3)

DO NOT WRITE IN THIS MARGIN

Marks KU PS

3. The grid shows the names of some hydrocarbons.

A methane	B hexane	C pentane
D ethene	E butene	F propane

(*a*) Identify the hydrocarbon with **six** carbon atoms in the molecule.

A	B	C
D	E	F

1

(*b*) Identify the **two** hydrocarbons which are alkenes.

A	B	C
D	E	F

1

(2)

[Turn over

DO NOT WRITE IN THIS MARGIN

Marks | KU | PS

4. The grid shows the names of some compounds.

A copper carbonate	B potassium sulphite
C sodium fluoride	D calcium sulphide

(*a*) Identify the compound which could be used as a fertiliser.

A	B
C	D

1

(*b*) Identify the compound which produces a yellow flame colour.

You may wish to use page 4 of the data booklet to help you.

A	B
C	D

1

(*c*) Identify the **two** compounds which contain oxygen.

A	B
C	D

1

(3)

DO NOT WRITE IN THIS MARGIN

Marks | KU | PS

5. A student made the following statements about chemical reactions.

A	A solid is always formed.
B	A gas is always produced.
C	There is always a colour change.
D	A new substance is always formed.

Identify the statement which is true for **all** chemical reactions.

A
B
C
D

(1)

[Turn over

DO NOT WRITE IN THIS MARGIN

Marks | KU | PS

6. The grid below shows the names of some oxides.

A iron oxide	B copper oxide	C potassium oxide
D calcium oxide	E lead oxide	F nitrogen dioxide

(*a*) Identify the oxide produced by the sparking of air in car engines.

A	B	C
D	E	F

1

(*b*) Identify the oxide which contains an alkali metal.

A	B	C
D	E	F

1

(*c*) Identify the oxide which dissolves in water to produce an acidic solution.

A	B	C
D	E	F

1

(3)

DO NOT WRITE IN THIS MARGIN

Marks | KU | PS

7. The grid shows some statements which can be applied to different solutions.

A	It has a pH of 7.
B	It reacts with silver.
C	It conducts electricity.
D	It produces chlorine when electrolysed.

(*a*) Identify the statement which is correct for water but **not** for dilute hydrochloric acid.

A
B
C
D

1

(*b*) Identify the statement which is correct for **both** dilute hydrochloric acid and dilute sulphuric acid.

A
B
C
D

1

(2)

[Turn over

DO NOT WRITE IN THIS MARGIN

Marks | KU | PS

8. The grid shows the names of some substances.

A argon	B crude oil	C sodium
D air	E carbon dioxide	F silicon

(*a*) Identify the **two** non-metal elements.

You may wish to use page 1 of the data booklet to help you.

A	B	C
D	E	F

1

(*b*) Identify the **two** mixtures.

A	B	C
D	E	F

2

(3)

DO NOT WRITE IN THIS MARGIN

Marks KU PS

PART 2

A total of 40 marks is available in this part of the paper.

9. Candle wax contains hydrocarbons.

(*a*) Name the elements present in a hydrocarbon.

____

____ **1**

(*b*) A student carried out the following experiment.

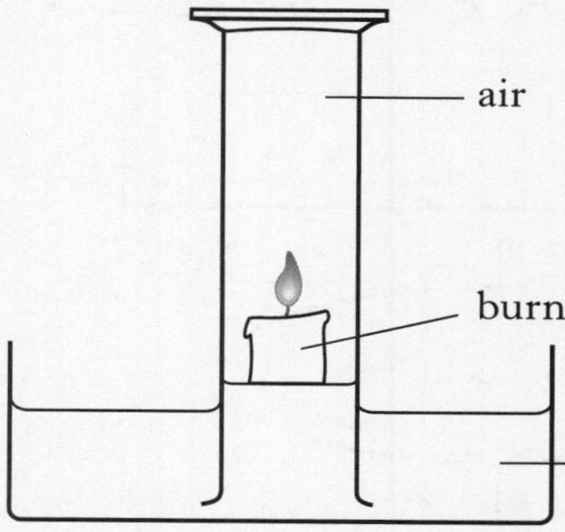

(i) Which gas is used up when a candle burns?

______________________________ **1**

(ii) In the experiment, a gas was produced which turned the lime water milky.

Name the gas produced.

______________________________ **1**

(3)

[Turn over

DO NOT WRITE IN THIS MARGIN

Marks KU PS

10. **PVC Production**

In the manufacture of PVC, ethylene and chlorine are passed through a catalyst chamber producing ethylene dichloride. The ethylene dichloride is then cracked to produce vinyl chloride which undergoes polymerisation to form the plastic poly(vinyl chloride), PVC.

(*a*) Use this information to complete the flow diagram.

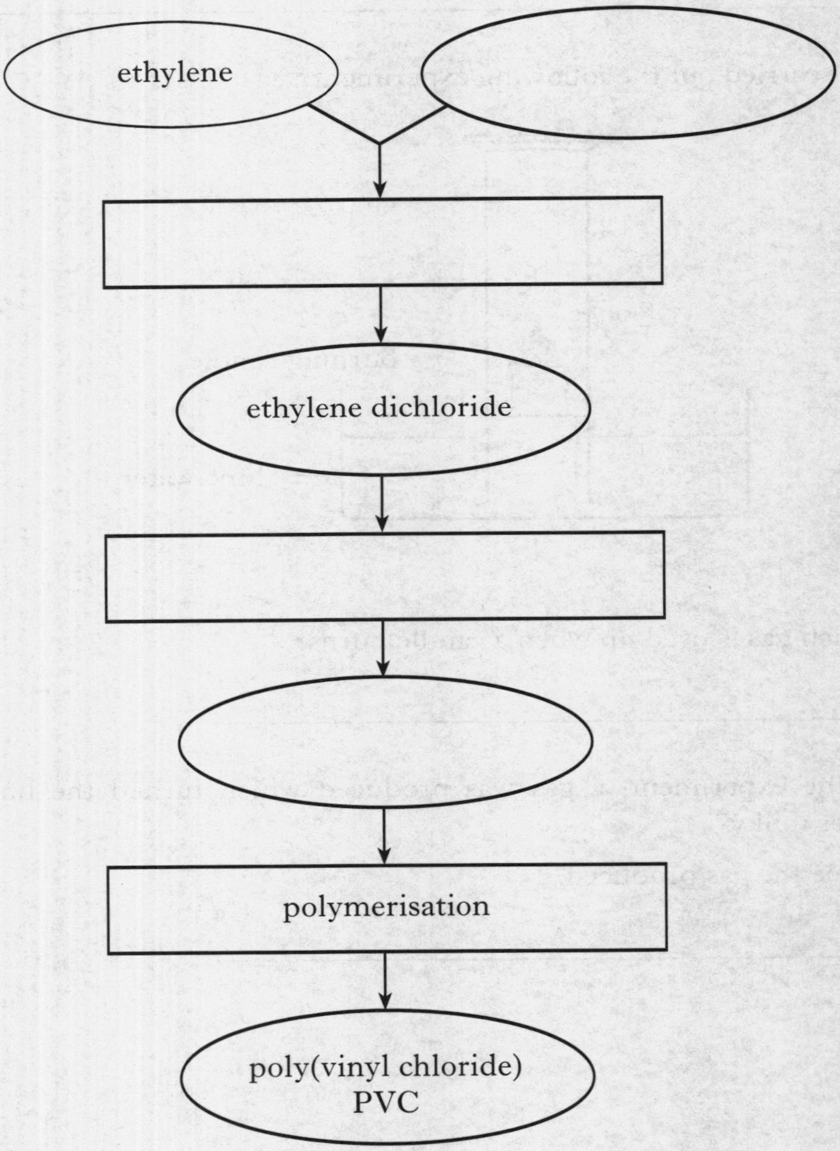

2

DO NOT WRITE IN THIS MARGIN

Marks | KU | PS

10. (continued)

(*b*) Plastics have many different uses. Poly(vinyl chloride) can be used to make clothes. The non-stick coating on saucepans is made from poly(tetrafluoroethene). Plastic bags are made from poly(ethene) while washing-up bowls are made from poly(propene).

Present this information as a table with suitable headings. **2**

(*c*) Name the monomer used to make poly(ethene).

_______________________________ **1**

(*d*) The graph shows the world production of plastics.

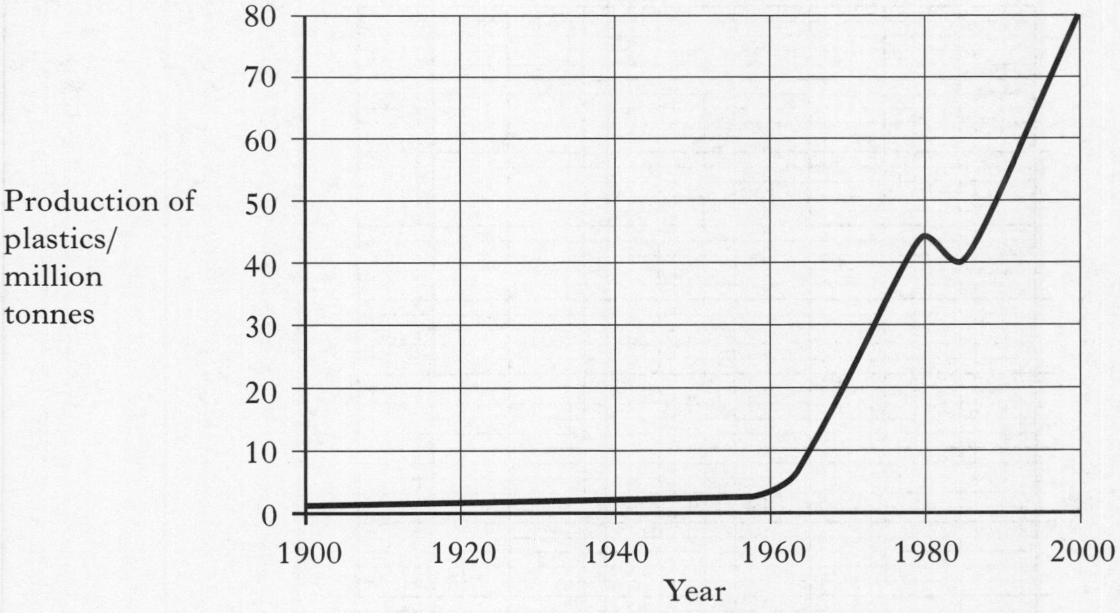

Describe the general trend in the production of plastics from 1960 to 2000.

____

_______________________________ **1**

(6)

DO NOT WRITE IN THIS MARGIN

Marks KU PS

11. The pie chart shows the uses of ethanoic acid.

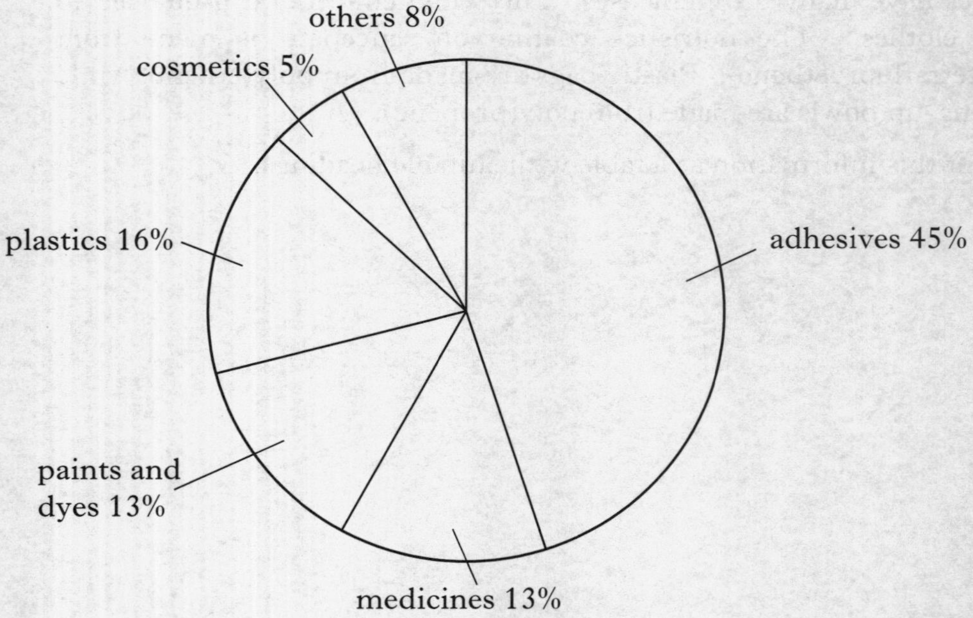

(*a*) Draw a bar graph to show the information in the pie chart.
Use appropriate scales to fill most of the graph paper.
(Additional graph paper, if required, can be found on page 23.)

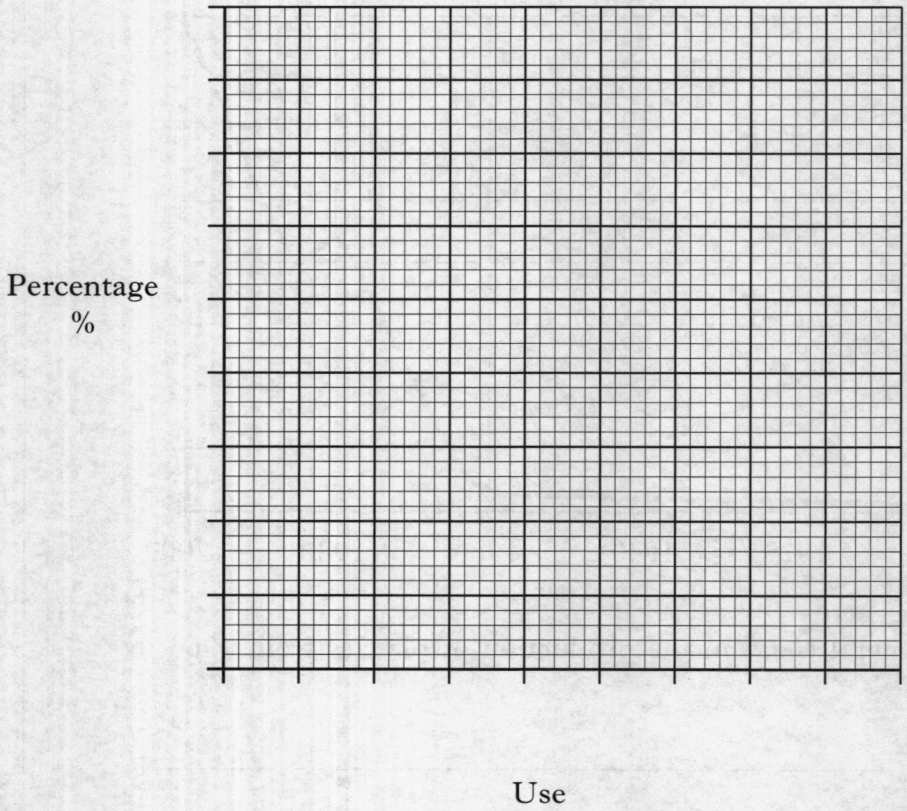

2

DO NOT WRITE IN THIS MARGIN

11. (continued) *Marks* KU PS

(*b*) The diagram shows a molecule of ethanoic acid.

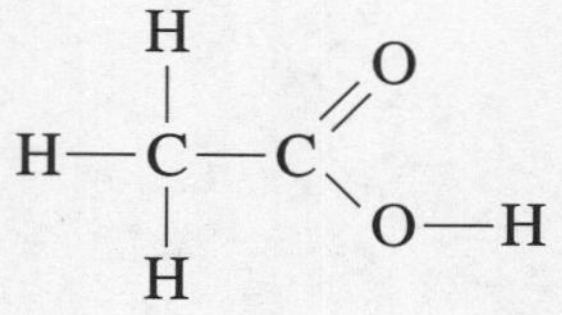

Write the molecular formula for ethanoic acid. **1**

(*c*) Describe how you would use universal indicator or pH paper to measure the pH of ethanoic acid solution.

____

____

______________________________ **1**

(*d*) Complete the sentence below by circling the correct answer.

Diluting an ethanoic acid solution with water will

increase
not change } the pH number. **1**
decrease

(*e*) Name the ion present in **all** acidic solutions.

______________________________ **1**

(6)

[Turn over

DO NOT WRITE IN THIS MARGIN

Marks KU PS

12. The Falkirk Wheel is a steel structure which carries boats from one level of the canal to another.

(*a*) The Falkirk Wheel is painted to prevent rusting.

How does painting prevent rusting?

____

____ **1**

(*b*) Suggest another method of preventing steel from rusting.

____ **1**

(*c*) (i) Steel is an alloy

What is meant by the term alloy?

____ **1**

(ii) The table gives information on the hardness of some steel alloys.

Carbon present in steel alloy/%	***Hardness/units***
0·1	123
0·2	157
0·3	190
0·4	220
0·5	260

Predict the hardness of a steel alloy containing 0·6% carbon.

________________ units **1**

(4)

DO NOT WRITE IN THIS MARGIN

Marks | KU | PS

13. Naveed carried out an experiment to investigate the reactivity of metals with dilute sulphuric acid.

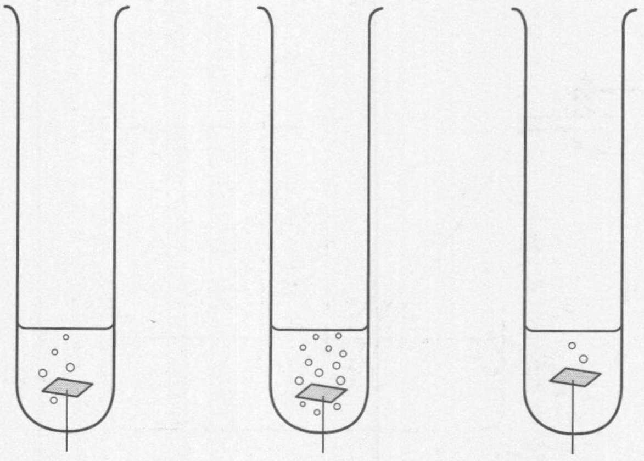

(*a*) Place the metals in order of reactivity (most reactive first).

____ **1**

(*b*) Name the gas produced when a metal reacts with dilute sulphuric acid.

____ **1**

(*c*) What would happen to the rate of the reaction if Naveed repeated the experiment using a higher concentration of sulphuric acid?

____ **1**

(3)

[Turn over

DO NOT WRITE IN THIS MARGIN

Marks | KU | PS

14. Cracking long-chain hydrocarbons produces smaller, more useful molecules.

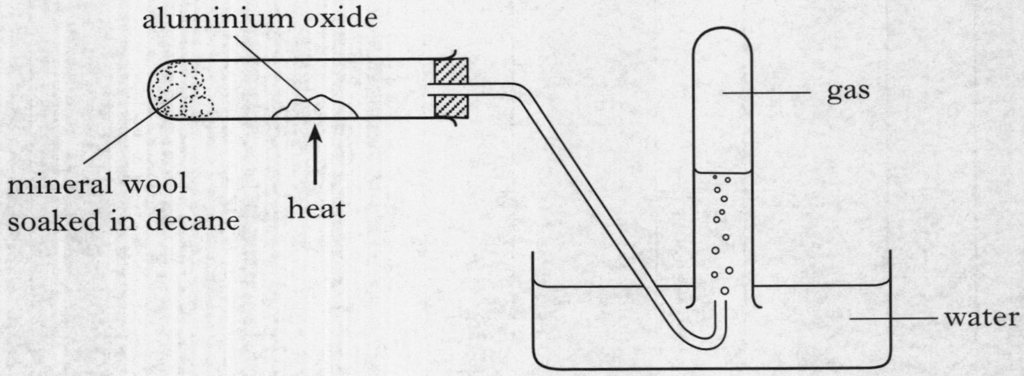

One of the reactions taking place is:

$$\underset{\text{decane}}{C_{10}H_{22}} \longrightarrow \underset{\text{octane}}{C_8H_{18}} + \mathbf{X}$$

(*a*) Draw a structural formula for octane. **1**

(*b*) (i) Write the molecular formula for **X**. **1**

(ii) **X** decolourises bromine solution.

What does this indicate about **X**?

____ **1**

(*c*) 0·1 g of aluminium oxide was used as a catalyst.

(i) What mass of aluminium oxide will be present at the end of the experiment?

________________ g **1**

(ii) Write the formula for aluminium oxide. **1**

(5)

DO NOT WRITE IN THIS MARGIN

Marks | KU | PS

15. A battery is a number of cells joined together.

(*a*) (i) Give **one** advantage of using a battery rather than mains electricity.

____

____ **1**

(ii) Why does a battery stop producing electricity after some time?

____

____ **1**

(*b*) A simple cell was set up as shown below.

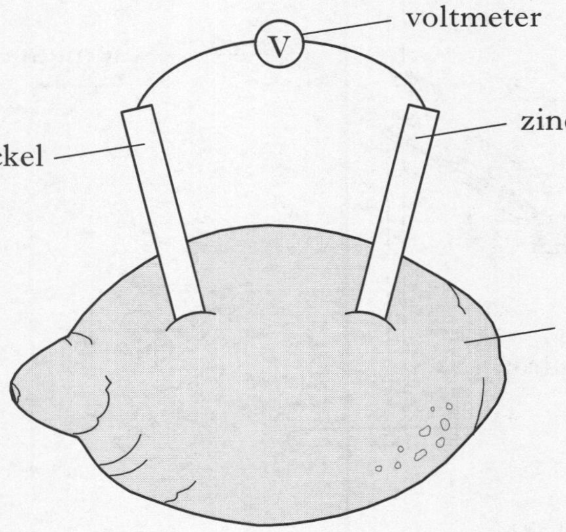

(i) Draw an arrow **on the wire** to show the direction of electron flow.

You may wish to use page 7 of the data booklet to help you. **1**

(ii) Would the voltage be higher **or** lower if the nickel were replaced by copper?

You may wish to use page 7 of the data booklet to help you.

____________________ **1**

(4)

[Turn over

DO NOT WRITE IN THIS MARGIN

Marks KU PS

16. Starch and sucrose are carbohydrates.

(*a*) Describe the chemical test, including the result, for starch.

____

____ **1**

(*b*) Starch is made by joining glucose molecules together.

Name the **type** of chemical reaction taking place.

____ **1**

(*c*) Harry set up an experiment to investigate the burning of carbohydrates.

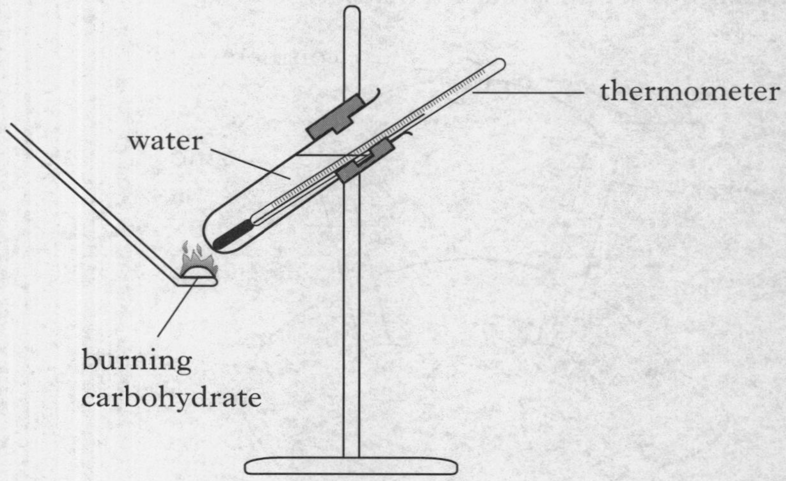

His results are shown below.

Carbohydrate	***Starting temperature of water/°C***	***Final temperature of water/°C***
starch	18	38
sucrose	18	52

DO NOT WRITE IN THIS MARGIN

Marks KU PS

16. (*c*) (continued)

(i) Which carbohydrate, starch or sucrose, released the most heat energy?

______________________________ **1**

(ii) Harry used the same volume of water in each experiment.

Suggest another variable which would have to be kept the same to make a fair comparison.

____ **1**

(*d*) Animals and plants obtain energy by breaking down carbohydrates.

Name this process.

___________________________________ **1**

(5)

[Turn over for Question 17 on *Page twenty-two*

DO NOT WRITE IN THIS MARGIN

	Marks	KU	PS

17. (*a*) A technician set up the following experiment to electrolyse molten lead iodide.

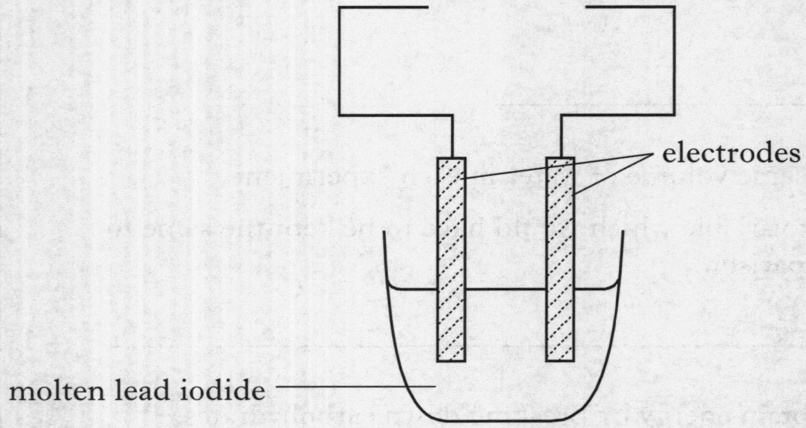

(i) In the diagram, the technician has left out a piece of apparatus needed to electrolyse molten lead iodide.

Name the piece of apparatus which has been left out of the circuit.

____ **1**

(ii) During electrolysis, the lead iodide is broken down into its elements.

Write a **word** equation for this reaction.

____ **1**

(*b*) Why do ionic compounds, like lead iodide, **not** conduct electricity when **solid**?

____

____

____ **1**

(*c*) Name the non-metal element which can be used as the electrodes.

____ **1**

(4)

[*END OF QUESTION PAPER*]

DO NOT WRITE IN THIS MARGIN

KU PS

ADDITIONAL SPACE FOR ANSWERS

ADDITIONAL GRAPH PAPER FOR QUESTION 11(*a*)

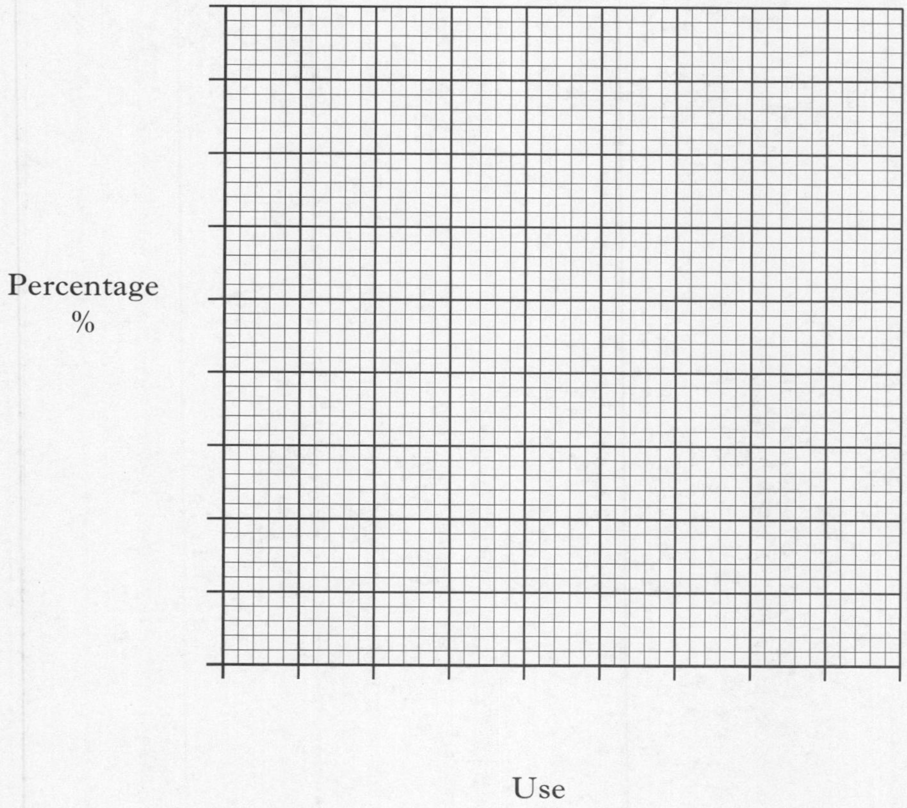

DO NOT WRITE IN THIS MARGIN

KU	PS

ADDITIONAL SPACE FOR ANSWERS

DO NOT WRITE IN THIS MARGIN

KU	PS

ADDITIONAL SPACE FOR ANSWERS

ADDITIONAL SPACE FOR ANSWERS

DO NOT WRITE IN THIS MARGIN

KU	PS

ADDITIONAL SPACE FOR ANSWERS

DO NOT WRITE IN THIS MARGIN

KU	PS

ADDITIONAL SPACE FOR ANSWERS

[BLANK PAGE]

[BLANK PAGE]